THE
TRUMP SURVIVAL GUIDE

WITHDRAWN

THE
TRUMP
SURVIVAL GUIDE

EVERYTHING YOU NEED TO KNOW ABOUT LIVING
THROUGH WHAT YOU HOPED WOULD NEVER HAPPEN

GENE STONE

WITH Nicholas Bromley, Tetsuhiko Endo, Mark Langley, Michael
Otterman, Kendra Pierre-Louise, Carl Pritzkat, Miranda Spencer

DEY ST.

An Imprint of WILLIAM MORROW

HarperCollins books may be purchased for educational, business, or sales promotional use. For information, please email the Special Markets Department at SPsales@harpercollins.com.

FIRST EDITION

Library of Congress Cataloging-in-Publication Data has been applied for.

ISBN 978-0-06-268648-0

17 18 19 20 21 RRD 10 9 8 7 6 5 4

*This book is dedicated to the American ideal
that our nation is governed by the majority
but never at the expense of the minority*

CONTENTS

THE
TRUMP SURVIVAL GUIDE

INTRODUCTION

On November 8, 2016, Donald J. Trump was elected president. Most of this book's readers probably didn't vote for him. In fact, for a great many Americans, his election was an unthinkable, unimaginable event. That doesn't matter now. It happened. Now all anyone can do is wait and see what kind of president Donald John Trump will become. On the hopeful side, he has not put forth a clear and consistent ideology, and some say this means he is simply the ultimate pragmatist. On the other side of the ledger, his pre-inauguration appointments do not signal pragmatism, and are giving many people cause for extreme concern. But as a FiveThirtyEight headline read after the election, "WE'VE NEVER KNOWN LESS ABOUT AN INCOMING PRESIDENT'S IDEOLOGY."

By itself, serving as president doesn't assure one historical greatness or even importance. And mouthing off in an unpleasant way doesn't necessarily do a nation serious long-term harm. Many American presidents have been deemed to have been failures or nonstarters. One of the most forgettable was John Tyler, the tenth president of the United States. He became president only because the ninth president, William Henry Harrison, died of the pneumonia he is said to have caught at his inauguration, thus giving Vice President Tyler the top job (and the nickname His Accidency). Tyler vetoed key points of his own Whig party's program, leading to the resignation of all but one member of his cabinet; was almost impeached; and was eventually discarded by the Whigs at the next election cycle. Teddy Roosevelt summed up his legacy this way: "Tyler has been called a mediocre man, but this is unwarranted flattery."

James Buchanan, the fifteenth president, was either equally ignorable (the defenders' view) or downright destructive (the detractors' view). He insisted that Congress had no power to stop the spread of slavery into the territories, and watched helplessly as the nation began to split apart. Now consider Warren G. Harding, who appointed dozens of corrupt officials to powerful positions, prompting perhaps the second-biggest scandal in White House history, the Teapot Dome bribery affair. And of course there's Richard M. Nixon, the instigator of the biggest scandal: the Watergate break-in and its cover-up. Nixon was the only president to be driven ignominiously from the White House in the midst of his term, resigning in 1974.

At the moment, historians aren't looking terribly kindly at George W. Bush either, since he may have committed the most serious foreign policy error in our nation's history: the second Gulf War.

Other presidents, having taken office surrounded by doubts, stepped up to the role. Abraham Lincoln was well respected, but little in his previous career suggested he would become the greatest president in our nation's history. Dwight Eisenhower—like Trump—came into the office without having ever having held a political office, but he earned a place on many historians' top-ten lists. Harry Truman is a classic growth story. He inherited the presidency upon Franklin D. Roosevelt's death and wasn't even expected to keep the job at the next election. He not only won, but is also widely deemed to have been an excellent commander in chief.

Presidents are best judged by history, decades after their administrations conclude. Thus it's difficult, and perhaps unfair, to judge Trump *before* his even begins. We don't know what he's going to do. His backstory is so murky and his disclosures so scanty that we don't even know much about what he's already done.

However, judging from his most extreme outbursts and his choice of inner circle, there are plenty of horrific possibilities. He could, for example, transfer power over all federal lands to the states, where their protection from development and environmental harm would become minimal. He could back out of all of the international climate change agreements—which would stun the rest of the participating nations. He could undo nearly a century of progress by appointing conservative justices, both to lower courts and to the Supreme Court, tilting the laws of the land rightward for decades to come. He could dismantle what little regulatory protection we currently have from the Wall Street excesses that caused the Great Recession. He could force us into some (doomed) armed foreign conflict, perhaps this time with Iran. He could roll back universality of health coverage, the proudest contribution of the outgoing president. And he could undo, even without legislation, many other aspects of the Obama legacy.

We don't know yet which, if any, of these paths Trump will take. If he turns out to be a moderate pragmatist, or his loud bark turns out to be worse than his cutting bite, then we will all have been worrying (or panicking) for naught. In that case, we will remember him as just another politician who didn't live up to either his campaign promises or our worst fears. That's the good case.

This book, however, is about how to deal with the bad case. If Trump and his team attempt to do grievous harm to the country, then it will be our duty to oppose him vigorously—in any legal, intelligent, thoughtful, practical way we can. It will do little good to continue the mutual demonizing and personalization that characterized this appalling recent campaign. Instead, we need to be disciplined and try to confine our attention to his actions.

We are not powerless. Keep in mind that although Trump

was elected, he won with the support of barely one-quarter of possible eligible voters. And he lost the popular vote. So if he does propose the policies we fear, everyone who voted against him and everyone who *should* have voted against him can join together, forming a healthy majority that can fight to stop his proposals. (A note to those who didn't vote: If you feel badly, the future offers you redemption. Make things right by joining the fight against destructive actions. That can be just as valuable as the vote you never cast.)

This book will give you the resources to do just that. Here you will find the background for twelve of the major issues facing the American public today: civil rights, the economy, education, energy, entitlement programs, the environment, immigration, LGBTQ issues, national security, Obamacare, political issues, and women's issues. Unless you remember your high school American history classes, most of this information has probably disappeared from your brain's memory banks. Consider this a refresher.

The book will also inform you as to President Obama's actions on these issues, and provide you with a preview of what Trump may (or may not) do. Most important, you will see suggestions to help you when (not if) you decide to become an active participant in our democracy by fighting firmly and proudly for your rights, your beliefs, and your country.

"A well-educated black has a tremendous advantage over a well-educated white in terms of the job market. . . . If I was starting off today, I would love to be a well-educated black, because I really do believe they have the actual advantage today."

—Donald Trump [1]

CIVIL RIGHTS

THE BACKGROUND

Before the Civil War, the concept of civil rights existed only as far as it concerned the rights of white Americans, a fact attested to by the Supreme Court's 1857 *Dred Scott* decision, which stated that anyone of African descent could never become a citizen of the United States and enjoyed "no rights which the white man was bound to respect." But throughout the nineteenth century, many other people whom we would now consider "white"—among them Italians, Slavs, and the Irish—were also the targets of discrimination, smeared in the press, denied entry to certain establishments, and generally stigmatized by the rest of society. (White-on-white prejudice was eventually diluted by successive waves of white migration around the country.)

Although there was a nascent abolitionist movement led mostly by free black Americans such as Frederick Douglass, and also white Americans such as William Lloyd Garrison, it took the Civil War and, subsequently, three new amendments to the Constitution (the Thirteenth, Fourteenth, and Fifteenth) to establish the right of black Americans to live as full citizens. In response, the ensuing century saw so-called Jim Crow policies sprout up like weeds around the country. By 1910, ten of the eleven former Confederate states passed new laws that effectively disenfranchised blacks through a combination of poll taxes, literacy tests, and many other restrictions. Most of these laws (named for a popular minstrel character of the time) were stemmed from the 1893 Supreme Court case *Plessy v. Ferguson*, which established the now-reviled idea of "separate but equal" institutions that were, indeed, separate but hardly equal.

From the late nineteenth century to the mid-twentieth century, white terrorism against nonwhite communities spiked and mass lynching was common across America. Approximately 4,000 lynchings of black citizens took place in the South between 1877 and 1950. A further 547 Mexicans (a growing minority at the time) were lynched between 1848 and 1928.

In 1909, black lawyers and activists led by W.E.B. Du Bois, Mary White Ovington, and Ida B. Wells founded the National Association for the Advancement of Colored People (NAACP) to raise awareness of discrimination against black Americans and combat it using the courts. But it wasn't until 1954 that the organization finally triumphed in one of the most important court cases of the era, *Brown v. Board of Education,* in which the Supreme Court declared school segregation unconstitutional, definitively overturning the *Plessy* precedent of "separate but equal."

Many states had no intention of desegregating their institutions without a fight. In response, the Southern Christian Leadership Conference, led by Dr. Martin Luther King Jr., organized protest movements across the South in the 1950s and '60s. With direct actions such as the Montgomery Bus Boycott, which was sparked by the civil disobedience of Rosa Parks, these activists demonstrated the power of nonviolent protest. They were joined by organizations including the Student Nonviolent Coordinating Committee, which organized the now-famous sit-ins at segregated lunch counters and the "Freedom Rides" through the Deep South to integrate segregated bus terminals.

Around the same time, the Chicano Civil Rights Movement, led by luminaries including Cesar Chavez and Reies López Tijerina, was also active. These activists worked to develop a pan-Latin identity for Latin Americans living in America and advocated fair wages and workers' rights. Although Latin Americans did not suffer the same style of deeply entrenched segregation suffered by black Americans, they were nonetheless systematically abused and struggled to survive on the wages paid to those on the bottom rungs of the labor ladder. They also suffered various mass deportations in the nine-teenth and twentieth centuries (see the Immigration chapter, page 91) that made their position in America feel precarious. On the East Coast, Puerto Ricans in cities like New York and Philadelphia also held demonstrations to protest unequal treatment.

The midcentury legal battles, political agitation, and orga-nized protests led to the landmark Voting Rights Act of 1964, which outlawed discriminatory voting practices and secured voting rights for racial minorities.

In the 1970s, the rise of Black Nationalist groups such as the Black Panthers, along with the decision of less militant civil rights organizations to focus their efforts on alleviating poverty in northern ghettos, alienated many white Americans who had preferred to quietly support Civil Rights from afar. Meanwhile, Richard Nixon rose to power on the back of an ascendant Republican party that had devised the "Southern Strategy"—a plan to siphon off old Southern Democrats, called Dixiecrats, who had grown disenchanted with their party by appealing to their deeply held racist sentiments. It worked well, and filled the Republican voter base with working-class whites from the South.

"The Nixon campaign in 1968, and the Nixon White House after that, had two enemies, the antiwar left and black people," Nixon's domestic policy chief, John Ehrlichman, told an interviewer not long ago.[2] "We knew we couldn't make it illegal to be either against the war or black, but by getting the public to associate the hippies with marijuana and blacks with heroin and then criminalizing both heavily, we could disrupt those communities. We could arrest their leaders, raid their homes, break up their meetings, and vilify them night after night on the evening news. Did we know we were lying about the drugs? Of course we did."

The criminalization of black people (males in particular) both in concept and in the heavy-handed enforcement of the so-called "War on Drugs" helped plant the seeds of systemic mass incarceration that exists today. Throughout the 1970s and '80s, discriminatory judicial practices including mandatory prison sentences have put a large number of black men in jail for relatively petty crimes. After being incarcerated, many are unable to vote or find gainful employment. As a result of what have been dubbed the new Jim Crow laws, the incarcerated population of the United States is now composed mostly of racial minorities. Although blacks and Latinos comprise only one-quarter of America's population, they account for about 60 percent of the country's prisoners.

After September 11, 2001, Muslim men also became targets of civil-rights violations when as many as 779 individuals were imprisoned at the Guantánamo Bay Naval Base during President Bush's "War on Terror." These detainees were denied their constitutional right of habeas corpus—that is, held without formal charges having been filed against them. Despite

President Obama's various promises to close the prison, sixty men remained imprisoned there.

WHAT DID BARACK OBAMA DO?

While Barack Obama has brought concern for all Americans to the White House, regardless of race, gender, or sexual orientation, he has left only a handful of tangible civil rights reforms, though many are extremely important.

Obama named the nation's first Latina woman justice to the Supreme Court: Sonia Sotomayor, a judge who had demonstrated a long-standing commitment to civil rights.

Although Obama has been criticized for not doing enough to address mass incarceration, he did sign into law the Fair Sentencing Act, which reduced the enormous sentencing disparities between people caught with crack cocaine versus powder cocaine.

Obama also signed the Hate Crimes Prevention Act, which greatly expanded the definition of hate crimes to include those based on sexual orientation, gender, and disability.

During the Obama years, killings of unarmed black men by police dominated the news cycle. In a speech given after the fatal shooting of the unarmed black teenager Trayvon Martin, Obama said, ". . . when Trayvon Martin was first shot I said that this could have been my son. Another way of saying that is Trayvon Martin could have been me thirty-five years ago."

These aren't just empty musings on Obama's part: In the last eight years, the civil rights division of his Justice Department has opened wide-ranging investigations of twenty-three police departments suspected of race-related violations.

As America's first black president, Obama has consistently engaged with the topic of race, helping to break the long-standing taboo that has developed around the subject in America. While we are not living in a post-racial world as many had hoped when he was first elected, we seem to have entered a new era of racial discourse in which movements like Black Lives Matter are pushing many old prejudices out into the open and forcing their examination.

WHAT MIGHT DONALD TRUMP DO?

Donald Trump ran his presidential campaign as a "law and order" candidate—a form of dog-whistle politics that, since Richard Nixon adopted it during his 1968 presidential campaign, has served as a veiled call for protecting white America. Throughout his candidacy, Trump was a vocal supporter of New York's arguably unconstitutional "Stop and Frisk" laws that targeted young black men; he also accused the Black Lives Matter movement of putting the lives of police officers at risk, claiming the organization is "essentially calling death to the police."[3]

Two of Trump's key appointments have been actively

lauded by white supremacists. The first, chief strategist Steve
Bannon, is the former head of Breitbart News Network, a website that became an outlet for racism, white nationalism, sexism, and anti-Muslim commentary. The second appointee is
the new attorney general, Jeff Sessions. In 1986, a Republican
Congress rejected Sessions' nomination for a position as a federal judge based on testimony by colleagues suggesting he was a
racist. Sessions opposed the Voting Rights Act of 1964 and as a
federal prosecutor brought charges against civil rights workers
trying to register black voters in rural Alabama. He has supported a ban on all Muslim immigration and proposed a campaign to arrest illegal immigrants that would raise the already
maxed-out prison population by a significant percentage.

WHAT YOU CAN DO

VOTE. Many of the policies related to our civil rights, such as access to education, unemployment benefits, prison reform, and
the right to vote, are legislated at the state level. This means
the people you elect to lead your state have a direct hand in
shaping them. Remember that it was state governments that
kept public schools segregated, even after the federal government ordered them integrated.

GET INVOLVED. Social justice organizations tend to collaborate, so
the key to hearing about protests and public actions regarding

civil rights is to get on the mailing lists of groups that are either directly involved with promoting civil rights in your area or affiliated with wider social-justice movements. Here are some of the major ones:

The Leadership Conference on Civil Rights: This coalition of civil rights organizations offers numerous resources for grassroots community organizing on its website. They also have a helpful newsletter that will help you get involved in the civil rights issues facing your area (www.civilrights.org).

Showing Up for Racial Justice: This organization is dedicated to organizing white Americans who want to help promote racial justice within their own communities. Aside from accepting volunteers for both skilled and unskilled positions, the group also offers advice and support on a wide range of topics, such as how to talk to your conservative relatives about issue of race and equality (www.showingupforracialjustice.org).

Black Lives Matter started as a hashtag but is now a chapter-based social movement organization that holds rallies and protests in places where police brutality has been in the headlines around the country. If you enjoy marches, teach-ins, and other direct action, consider supporting this organization (www.blacklivesmatter.com).

Meetup.com: This site, which helps you find people with similar hobbies in your area, is a great place to find home-grown social justice and civil-rights groups. By simply clicking on the "Movements" tile on their front page, you will be directed to a list of social justice groups near you (www.meetup.com).

DONATE TO ORGANIZATIONS. The NAACP Legal Defense Fund fought many of the biggest legal battles that the Civil Rights Movement faced in the 1950s and 1960s, and it is still fighting them today (www.naacpldf.org).

The Mexican American Legal Defense and Education Fund litigates for immigrant rights and voting rights for Latinos, the most rapidly growing ethnic group in the country. If Trump implements the coercive deportation tactics he campaigned on, this group will likely be on the front lines of defending Latin Americans' civil rights (www.maldef.org).

The Anti-Defamation League is an international organization founded in 1913 to fight anti-Semitism and all other forms of bigotry. This group, which has been criticized recently for some of its international actions, has been monitoring the recent sharp increase in anti-Semitic outbursts in the United States since the election (www.adl.org).

REPORT HATE CRIMES. An unreported hate crime is an invisible hate crime; violence and oppression are most dangerous when they exist in the shadows. Whether you witness racist abuse or simply see hateful words scrawled in graffiti, alert the police. They keep statistics on hate crimes that advocacy groups around the country use in their media and when lobbying Washington.

PRACTICE ALLY-SHIP AND DEVELOP AWARENESS OF INTERSECTIONALITY. An "ally" is someone who is not a person of color but who wishes to empower other people who are. It requires educating yourself about the racist history of the United States and then looking for ways in which you can support your friends in their quest for justice. It also means fostering relationships and forming alliances across the boundaries that have historically divided Americans. Actions can range from becoming the pen pal of a prisoner to inviting your Arab-American neighbor over for coffee.

INTERSECTIONALITY, a term coined by law professor Kimberle Crenshaw in the 1980s, describes the multiple types of discrimination individuals can face because they are members of several minority classes at once—say, your coworker who is an immigrant black woman or your relative who is both disabled and gay. The best way to be an ally and understand intersectionality is to expand your network among people who are not like you!

BOOKS TO READ

Between the World and Me by Ta-nehisi Coates (Spiegel and Grau, 2015). Written as a series of essays in a letter to

Coates' son, an explanation of the current state of racism
and police oppression toward black people in the U.S.

Covering: The Hidden Assault on Our Civil Rights by Kenji Yoshino
(Random House, 2007). Part legal manifesto, part memoir,
a call for a redefinition of civil rights in law and culture.

From #BlackLivesMatter to Black Liberation by Keeanga-
Yamahtta Taylor (Haymarket Books, 2016). A forceful,
well-written analysis of the struggle against police
brutality.

The New Jim Crow: Mass Incarceration in the Age of Colorblindness
by Michelle Alexander (The New Press, 2012). An
argument that our current criminal justice system acts as
a form of racial control.

Why We Can't Wait by Martin Luther King (Signet, 2000).
Dr. King's powerful 1964 classic that espouses love and
nonviolent direct action to achieve freedom and equality.

"I've done very well with debt. Now, of course I was swashbuckling, and it did well for me, and it was good for me and all of that. And you know debt was always sort of interesting to me. Now we're in a different situation with a country, but I would borrow knowing that if the economy crashed you could make a deal. And if the economy was good it was good so therefore you can't lose. It's like you make a deal before you go into a poker game. And your odds are much better."

—Donald Trump[1]

THE ECONOMY

THE BACKGROUND

The size, composition, and health of the U.S. economy has fluctuated dramatically over its history, but it has always been defined by one goal: growth.

After the American Revolution, most Americans lived on small farms and grew their own food. The cash economy was based primarily on shipbuilding and exports of tobacco, rice, and indigo. Alexander Hamilton, the nation's first secretary of the Treasury, successfully federalized the states' war debt to help build strong national credit and established the country's first national bank, leading to expanded shipping, manufacturing, and international commerce.

With the construction of canals and the introduction of steamboats and railroads, the economy grew larger and westward. Boosted by innovations such as the cotton gin, the South became saturated with plantations of varying size and profitability (albeit relying on slave labor). From northern shipbuilding and banking to southern cotton to western sugar cane, the United States economy was diversifying and expanding at a rapid pace. Mass industrialization spread, and by the time Abraham Lincoln was elected president, around a third of the country's income came from manufacturing and almost 20 percent of the population lived in cities. The Union victory over a decimated Confederacy in the Civil War heralded the country's continuing shift from an agrarian to an industrial economy.

The late nineteenth century was the age of the tycoon, from John D. Rockefeller's vast oil monopoly to Andrew Carnegie's steel empire to J.P. Morgan's ornate banks. With limited regulations, the U.S. economy was a roller coaster of booms and busts fueled by splendid machines, smoke-belching factories, and a high tide of political corruption. This era, known as the Gilded Age, was also defined by vast inequality. While the Progressive Era (1890–1920) ushered in anti-corruption legislation and the dismantling of monopolies, income inequality remained stubbornly high: In 1928, the richest 1 percent of families still controlled 24 percent of all pretax income.

The Great Depression, triggered by a stock market crash and numerous bank failures, moderated this inequality, wiping out savings and extravagant incomes among the rich, bringing them closer to parity with the already penniless poor. With high taxes following World War II—the top marginal tax rate reached 91 percent—the richest 1 percent's share of wealth tumbled to 11.3 percent and remained there for the next three decades, a time characterized by a booming economy and an expanding middle class. However, substantial tax cuts for the rich and financial deregulation under President Ronald Reagan in the mid-1980s, and more under President George W. Bush in the early 2000s, brought inequality back to Gilded Age levels. This trend continues unabated today.

And then disaster struck. At the end of Bush's second term, the United States was hit by the largest economic downturn since the Great Depression. While no one single factor caused it, a combination of reckless housing lending, a lack of financial regulation, and a general housing, asset, and credit bubble produced an extreme overhang of debt among businesses and families alike. Catastrophe loomed. Millions of Americans were losing their homes. Banks and securities firms were in danger failing due to overexposure to risky side bets based on subprime loans. In his final months in office, Bush authorizing a controversial $700 billion bailout package for the largest banks.

WHAT DID BARACK OBAMA DO?

On a frigid day in January 2009, President Obama inherited a nation in crisis. The unemployment rate was at 7.8 percent and rising fast as the economy lost hundreds of thousands of jobs per month. Credit had dried up, and consumers refused to spend.

In February 2009, supported by a fresh Democratic majority in both houses of Congress, Obama signed into law the American Recovery and Reinvestment Act, a $787 billion stimulus package designed to jumpstart the economy. The president had doubters on both sides of the aisle: Conservatives complained about the deficit impact, while liberals complained that the stimulus was not large enough. Nevertheless, history seems to be on Obama's side. As reported by the *Washington Post*:

- Gross domestic product (GDP) and total employment had been at historic lows and still falling. Both turned around almost immediately when the stimulus passed.
- The Congressional Budget Office determined that GDP in the fourth quarter of 2009 was up to 3.8 percent higher than it would have been without the stimulus.
- By the end of 2010, the economy supported 2.5 million jobs that would not have existed without the stimulus.
- The stimulus kept almost six million Americans out of poverty in 2009, according to the Center on Budget and Policy Priorities.

The stimulus package extended unemployment benefits, cut taxes, and funded public works projects around the country. Within seven months, the stimulus had pumped $242 billion into the economy, and by early 2010 economic growth had reached 3.9 percent. Republicans continued to protest that the stimulus would bankrupt the country, but the Center on Budget and Policy Priorities concluded that it would add only 3 percent to the existing budget shortfall through 2050.

Obama next turned his attention to the collapsing auto industry. For years, automakers had relied on gas-guzzling SUVs and trucks to undergird their business, but sales had plummeted with record gas prices and a frugal recession mentality gripping the nation. The struggling car companies could not meet their debt obligations. President Bush had agreed in December 2008 to temporarily bail out Chrysler and General Motors, but this stopgap measure was designed to keep the companies solvent for only a matter of months. Many prominent Republicans suggested that the companies should go through bankruptcy. Mitt Romney, whose father, George, was once president of the American Motors Company, penned an op-ed titled "Let Detroit Go Bankrupt."

The Obama administration determined that the economy could not risk the job losses if the auto industry were allowed to undergo bankruptcy, not to mention the psychological blow of watching two iconic American brands crumble. The federal government extended billions of dollars in loans, encouraged a merger for Chrysler with the Italian automaker Fiat, and assumed a 60 percent stake in General Motors. The companies returned to profitability in 2010 and the Treasury recouped $70.5 billion of the original $80.7 bailout. The revitalized auto industry has been central to the economic recovery, representing a quarter of all manufacturing gains.

On July 21, 2010, Obama signed into law the Dodd–Frank Wall Street Reform and Consumer Protection Act, tightening regulation in some of the areas that had led to the financial crisis. Criticized by the right as overregulation, and by the left as failing to deal with the larger issues (such as hedge fund disclosure and bank derivatives leverage), Dodd–Frank increased capital requirements for banks, created the Consumer Financial Protection Agency to regulate the issuance of credit cards and mortgages, and imposed the Volcker Rule, which prohibits commercial banks from making certain speculative bets with customer money.

Obama ended his second term with the economy on sound footing. He cut the deficit by 71 percent, largely by phasing out the stimulus program and increasing taxes on the wealthiest Americans. One projection has the debt-to-GDP ratio falling by more than half by 2046. In addition, Obama oversaw seventy-four consecutive months of private-sector job growth and nearly eighty straight months of economic expansion. Unemployment dropped from a high of 10 percent in October 2009, to 4.6 percent in December 2016. The stock market rebounded and repeatedly set new highs. Republicans blame Obama for vastly increasing the size of government, but federal spending under his watch increased by an average of only 3.3 percent annually—the lowest rate since the Eisenhower administration. Most important, since early 2010, the Obama administration presided over the creation of fifteen million jobs.

WHAT MIGHT DONALD TRUMP DO?

Trump has suggested that he might try to renegotiate the U.S. federal debt, making statements that were "neither clear nor coherent," according to Paolo Mauro, a senior fellow at the generally conservative Peterson Institute for International Economics.[2]

Granted, in the private sector, debt renegotiation is routine for troubled companies. Trump himself renegotiated a $30 million tax bill owed to the state of New Jersey down to just $5 million. (Interestingly, this occurred in 2011, the year after Trump ally Chris Christie became governor.) During the early 1990s, three of Trump's Atlantic City casinos filed for bankruptcy and his creditors agreed to forgive hundreds of millions of dollars in debt. Later, Trump used his losses to avoid paying federal income tax for nearly twenty years.

But renegotiating *government* debt is entirely different.

Trump's suggestion that he could ask creditors to accept less than 100 percent of what they are owed—a tactic historically employed by dysfunctional small nations and teetering dictatorships—could be devastating for the United States, the world's largest economy. The government is able to borrow money at extremely low interest rates because Treasury securities are regarded as the safest investment on the planet. As the *New York Times* reported, "Any cracks in investor confidence have a long history of costing American taxpayers a lot of money."[3] While Trump will not likely try this tactic, even the slightest suggestion that a sitting president would not pay our creditors what they are owed could cost taxpayers billions in increased interest rates for decades to come.

On the campaign trail, Trump promised to "massively cut taxes for the middle class, the forgotten people, the forgotten men and women of this country, who built our country."[4] When asked during a town hall meeting if he supported raising taxes on the rich, Trump replied: "I do. I do—including myself. I do."[5]

So is Trump truly a modern-day Robin Hood?

Not quite. According to Lily Batchelder, a visiting fellow at the Tax Policy Center, under Trump "the top 1 percent would get about half of the benefits of his tax cuts, and a millionaire, for example, would get an average tax cut of $317,000."[6] How about those massive tax cuts for the forgotten men and women who built this country? A family earning between $40,000 and $50,000 a year would see a tax cut of only $560, while "a single parent who's earning $75,000 and has two school-age children . . . would face a tax increase of over $2,400," according to Batchelder.

How good would these tax cuts be for the economy as a whole? The Tax Policy Center calculated that "the federal debt would rise by at least $7.2 trillion over the first decade and by at least $20.9 trillion by 2036."[7] According to an analysis by the University of Pennsylvania's Wharton School in collaboration with the Tax Policy Center, "In the long run, the Trump tax plan increases federal debt more than current policy, resulting in less economic growth."[8]

Can Trump realistically pass his plan? Don't bet against it. While most legislation requires a sixty-vote majority to overcome a Senate filibuster, the tax code can be amended through a process called budget reconciliation, which requires only a simple majority. This is how President Bush pushed his 2001 and 2003 tax cuts through Congress. (Tax cuts passed through reconciliation are not permanent. By Senate rules, they must be reauthorized in ten years.)

Maybe he won't get everything he wants. What if Trump chooses to take up House Speaker Paul Ryan's tax plan, which is more modest? By 2025, according to the Tax Policy Center, 99.6 percent of Ryan's tax cuts would benefit the richest 1 percent of Americans, with an average annual savings of $240,000. As the *Washington Post* reported, "The poorest 20 percent of

Americans would see an average increase of 0.5 percent in their incomes, or about $120 a year. Households in the upper middle class, those in the 60th percentile through the 95th percentile, would pay more in taxes on average."[9] All told, the plan could add as much as $4 trillion to the national debt over ten years.

TRUMP ON TRADE

Ripping up trade deals was a key plank of candidate Donald Trump's platform, a message that resonated in traditionally Democratic states with large working-class populations such as Michigan and Pennsylvania, which have seen manufacturing jobs shipped overseas. For one thing, Trump has promised to bring these jobs back by undoing the North American Free Trade Agreement (NAFTA), which was proposed by President George H.W. Bush and later ratified in 1993 by Congress and President Bill Clinton. The goal of NAFTA was to eliminate trade barriers between the United States, Canada, and Mexico, allowing goods to flow between borders without taxes on imports, known as tariffs. NAFTA was so controversial when it was proposed that a billionaire outsider presidential candidate named Ross Perot surged in the polls while railing against it. (Sound familiar?) Since NAFTA passed, trade with Canada and Mexico has tripled. Many manufacturing jobs have left America, but largely to countries overseas, such as China, so it is difficult to say how many jobs NAFTA has cost Americans. (One estimate by the Economic Policy Institute pegs the figure at several hundred thousand.) Trump has also threatened to tear up the Trans-Pacific Partnership (TPP), a trade agreement with twelve of the Pacific Rim countries that has not yet been ratified.

According to a memo from Trump's transition team, "The Trump administration will reverse decades of conciliatory trade policy. New trade agreements will be negotiated that provide for the interests of U.S. workers and companies first." [10] Trump has repeatedly said he would withdraw the country from the proposed TPP—"another disaster done and pushed by special interests who want to rape our country, just a continuing rape of our country" [11]—and will likely do so. Withdrawing from NAFTA —"the worst trade deal maybe ever signed anywhere" [12]—is trickier, but entirely possible. The United States has not withdrawn from a trade deal since 1866, but it is possible that all Trump needs to do is provide written notice to our trade partners. It's not clear what would happen next, but Gary Horlick, a trade lawyer, predicted that "U.S. importers would take the U.S. to court the next day." [13]

While Canadian prime minister Justin Trudeau has signaled he would be "more than happy to talk about" renegotiating NAFTA, Mexico is not so enthusiastic. [14] Backing out of NAFTA would require that American businesses spend enormous sums of money reorganizing (or re-reorganizing) their supply chains. Withdrawing could also incite a trade war by provoking Mexico into raising their own import tariffs. Considering we export $235 billion in goods every year to Mexico, some, including the Peterson Institute, feel that a trade war could cause a significant economic downturn and a spike in the U.S. unemployment rate.

Trump has threatened to impose a 45 percent tariff on China and a 35 percent tariff on Mexico. The latter plan could be devastating for some American companies. For example, Ford would owe $2.8 billion in import taxes—more than its most recent quarterly profit. While tariffs must normally be authorized by Congress, the president has the ability to enact unlimited tariffs in the event of a "national emergency," though such an action would likely end up in court. According to the Peterson Institute, imposing these tariffs would represent a "full trade war" and could possibly result in the nation losing "nearly 4.8 million private sector jobs," which would "inflict disproportionate hardship on low-skill, low-income workers." [15]

There is a legitimate issue about the way trade deals and treaties have been negotiated to date. Trump was joined by Bernie Sanders and Hillary Clinton during the campaign in criticizing the TPP. The terms have often been designed with little attention to worker conditions and environmental impact, allowing countries with the lowest standards to gain a competitive advantage. And the loss of American jobs has come more quickly than many can deal with, given the inertia of geographic mobility and the time it takes to retrain workers. Increased trade can be good, but dropping barriers too quickly can be painful and even counterproductive.

WHAT YOU CAN DO

STAY INFORMED. More than ever, it is crucial to rely on expert, nonpartisan analysis to understand what Trump's tax and trade plans mean for you and your family. Budget deficits and twelve-figure numbers can be difficult to parse, but reputable organizations can break down Trump's economic proposals into information that matters to you, such as important deductions and credits that may affect your taxes. In a time of fake news and unreliable information, here are some excellent organizations you should follow, and if possible, donate to:

The Tax Policy Center. A joint venture of the Urban Institute and the Brookings Institute, the Tax Policy Center aims to provide independent analyses of current and longer-term tax issues and to communicate its analyses to the public and to policymakers in a timely and accessible manner. The Center combines top national experts in tax, expenditure, budget policy, and microsimulation modeling to concentrate on overarching areas of tax policy that are critical to future debate (www.taxpolicycenter.org).

The Committee for a Responsible Federal Budget. The Committee for a Responsible Federal Budget is a nonpartisan, nonprofit organization committed to educating the public on issues with significant fiscal policy impact. The Committee's leadership comprises some of the nation's leading budget experts, including many past heads of the House and Senate Budget Committees, the Congressional Budget Office, the Office of Management and Budget, the Government Accountability Office, and the Federal Reserve Board. As an independent source of objective policy analysis, the Committee regularly engages policymakers of both parties to help them develop and analyze proposals to improve the country's fiscal and economic condition (www.crfb.org).

The Center for American Progress. The Center for American Progress (CAP) is an independent, nonpartisan policy institute dedicated to improving the lives of all Americans through bold, progressive ideas, as well as strong leadership and concerted action. CAP has published numerous studies detailing precisely how Trump's policies will affect Americans at all income levels (www.americanprogress.org).

BOOKS TO READ

The Conscience of a Liberal by Paul Krugman (Norton, 2009). A lesson in economic history by a Nobel Laureate, offering a defense of liberalism while showing how conservatism drove economic inequality.

After the Music Stopped: The Financial Crisis, the Response, and the Work Ahead by Alan S. Blinder (Penguin Books, 2013). An essential history of the financial crisis and how we can prevent another one.

The Price of Inequality: How Today's Divided Society Endangers Our Future by Joseph E. Stiglitz (Norton, 2013). How the wealthiest have "stifled true, dynamic capitalism" and driven inequality to record highs, by a Nobel Laureate.

Beyond Outrage: Expanded Edition: What Has Gone Wrong with Our Economy and Our Democracy, and How to Fix It by Robert B. Reich (Vintage, 2012). A roadmap showing what must be done to keep Washington in check and working for all Americans.

"We're twenty-sixth in the world. Twenty-five countries are better than us at education. And some of them are like third-world countries. But we're becoming a third-world country. . . . "

—Donald Trump [1]

EDUCATION

THE BACKGROUND

Almost two centuries ago, James Madison wrote that "A popular Government without popular information, or the means of acquiring it, is but a prologue to a farce or a tragedy, or perhaps both. Knowledge will forever govern ignorance. And a people who *mean* to be their own Governors, must arm themselves with the power which *knowledge* gives." The words were an appeal for the development of a national, free public education system.

Publicly funded schools did exist in colonial times and in our nation's early years, but most were run by churches. For example, Boston Latin School, the nation's first public school, was founded in 1635 by Puritans who placed a strong emphasis on literacy (primarily to enable Bible reading) and funded mostly by donations. The federal government left control of schools to the states, and states in turn largely left the task up to towns. This patchwork system worked in wealthier enclaves of the country, but too many children were being left behind. The first true champion for universal, nonsecular public education was Horace Mann (1796–1859). A member of the Whig Party, Mann served as secretary of the Massachusetts State Board of Education, and later as a member of Congress. Mann believed that mandatory education was the only way to turn American children into model citizens. As secretary, Mann personally inspected every school in Massachusetts and instituted reforms based on the Prussian model of "common schools" whereby teachers were professionally trained and all students received the same quality of education regardless of wealth. Mann's reforms were so popular that in 1852 Massachusetts passed a law requiring all children to attend school, and New York followed the next year. By 1918, with Mississippi finally falling in line, every state required children to attend at least grammar school.

While every child was guaranteed an education, they were not all guaranteed an *equal* education. An 1896 Supreme Court case, *Plessy v. Ferguson*, upheld the right of states to segregate public facilities. Public schools could be separated by race as long as they were "equal," but in practice this was rarely the case. It was not until 1954 that the Supreme Court finally ended state-sponsored segregation with the landmark case *Brown v. Board of Education*. Writing for the unanimous court, Chief Justice Earl Warren declared that "separate educational

facilities are inherently unequal," touching off the long, painful process of integrating the nation's schools. This is still ongoing, even in the most unlikely places. New York State, for
example, is considered by some measures to have the most seg-
regated·schools in America.

In 1979, President Jimmy Carter promoted the Office of
Education, which had steadily increased in size and scope
with President Lyndon Johnson's Great Society anti-poverty
programs, to the Department of Education (ED). Republicans
were largely opposed to the ED, complaining it was an unconstitutional bureaucratic intrusion into state-run programs.
The ED is the smallest cabinet-level department, with only
five thousand employees, and even with federal oversight, education in the United States remains highly decentralized. For
the most part, states set their own curricula and standards,
while giving local districts and school boards extensive auton-
omy over how to implement them.

Efforts to exert federal control over schools have yielded
mixed results. In 2001, under President George W. Bush, Congress passed the No Child Left Behind Act, which introduced
standards-based education reform. States were required to develop basic skills assessments, and federal funding for schools
was tied to how well students performed. The law was deeply
unpopular among liberals and conservatives alike. School districts complained that the law's expectations were unrealis-
tic, teachers complained about the emphasis on standardized

tests, and deficit hawks complained that the increase in federal education spending—from \$42.2 billion in 2001 to \$55.7 billion in 2004—was fiscally irresponsible.

Fundamental inequalities remain with public schools. Because schools are funded primarily by local property taxes, wealthy neighborhoods have much better facilities than low-income ones. In a given county, one school might have an Olympic-size swimming pool, offer advanced-placement courses, and have a Jumbotron on its athletic field, while the school down the road has a leaky roof and textbooks from the 1970s. Meanwhile, low-income schools are more likely to have inexperienced teachers. The latest edition of the "Is School Funding Fair?" report card found that numerous states grant *less* funding to school districts with higher concentrations of low-income students than they do to districts that are better off. This uneven support and varying quality has resulted in fifteen-year-olds in the United States ranking near the bottom out of sixty-five countries in mastery of math, science, and reading according to the Organisation for Economic Co-operation and Development's 2012 Program for International Student Assessment.

Although a large number of the world's top universities are in the United States, they are unaffordable for many families. In 1979, a student working a minimum-wage job for 385.5 hours (about ten weeks) could pay off one year of the average college tuition. Today, that figure is 2,229 hours, and 68 percent of college students graduate with debt averaging $30,100.

WHAT DID BARACK OBAMA DO?

By design, the education system in the United States is largely left to the states to administer, so it is difficult for a president to introduce top-down reforms. However, the Obama Administration managed to introduce numerous programs to help equalize opportunity for students nationwide, including:

The Every Student Succeeds Act. In 2015, under pressure from all sides, the No Child Left Behind Act was replaced with the Every Student Succeeds Act. While some standards remain from the previous program, the one-size-fits-all model was scrapped in favor of granting states flexibility to administer testing and teacher assessments. Every Student Succeeds passed with the support of 86 percent of House members and 88 percent of senators.

Race to the Top, a competitive grant program that rewards school districts that come up with innovative programs around standards and assessments, create innovative data systems to support instruction, and turn around the lowest performing schools, among many other criteria. To date, Race to the Top has dedicated more than $4 billion to nineteen states. Somewhat controversially, Race to the Top also pressured states to expand charter schools, which are publically funded, privately run independent schools that operate with more autonomy than traditional public schools.

Common Core guidelines. Common Core standards are descriptions of basic skills that students should have achieved at each grade level in English/language arts and mathematics. With the blessing of the Obama Administration, governors and state school superintendents developed the Common Core guidelines to ensure children receive a basic level of skills nationwide. Obama encouraged states to join by offering federal Race to the Top dollars for states that participated. Today, forty-two states and the District of Columbia have embraced Common Core Standards.

The REPAYE program. To provide student debt relief, the Department of Education under Obama passed the Revised Pay as You Earn (REPAYE) plan. For Department of Education–owned college loans, monthly payments are capped at 10 percent of the borrower's income. After twenty years of payments (or twenty-five years for graduate-school loans), the remaining balance is forgiven.

America's College Promise, a program, yet to be implemented, that would restructure community colleges to create better training in line with employer needs and current job demands while also providing free or reduced-cost two-year higher education to students who attend college at least half-time, maintain a 2.5 grade point average, and show steady progress toward completing their degree. The bill, introduced in 2015, has not yet been passed by Congress.

WHAT MIGHT DONALD TRUMP DO?

As Emily Deruy wrote in *The Atlantic,* "The short answer to the complicated question about what education looks like under Trump is: No one knows for sure."[2]

Trump (who recently settled a $25 million lawsuit related to alleged fraudulent activities by his now-defunct Trump University real-estate school) has said he would "cut the Department of Education,"[3] although doing so would be very difficult. However, Trump could drastically scale back ED oversight or direct its resources toward a longtime Republican goal: expanding private school vouchers. Under certain circumstances, children can receive special subsidies, or vouchers, to attend private or parochial schools. Trump has proposed providing a $20 billion block grant for such a program. Vouchers are controversial because they can blur the boundary between church and state if federal voucher dollars flow to religious schools instead of secular public schools.

Trump's choice for secretary of education, the billionaire Betsy DeVos, is a vocal advocate of school choice. In a 2013 interview, DeVos said that she is "most focused on educational choice. But, thinking more broadly, what we are trying to do is tear down the mind-set that assigns students to a school based solely on the ZIP code of their family's home. We advocate instead for as much freedom as possible."[4] DeVos is the former chairwoman of the Michigan Republican Party, where she led the crusade for school choice. As National Public Radio reported, "DeVos has helped make Michigan's charter schools among the least regulated in the nation. Some 80 percent of the state's charters are run by private companies." DeVos has zero public school experience—in fact, as *Forbes* noted, she has "reportedly never been part of a public school as a teacher or staff member or sent her children to one."[5]

Trump has also said, "Common Core is a total disaster. We can't let it continue."[6] However, Trump cannot simply do away with Common Core, since the standards were drafted and approved by the states. But he could redirect Race to the Top funding to create a disincentive for states to adhere to Common Core guidelines.

Trump has also threatened to dismantle the Office for Civil Rights (OCR), which enforces federal civil-rights laws prohibiting discrimination in programs or activities that receive federal financial assistance from the Department of Education. Eradicating the OCR would leave states with little oversight, despite the fact that black students are already less likely to be placed in gifted programs even if they have the same test scores as white students.

WHAT YOU CAN DO

JOIN AN ORGANIZATION THAT WORKS TO IMPROVE EDUCATION. Education Reform Now (edreformnow.org) has chapters in thirteen states, and Students for Education Reform (www.studentsfored reform.org) is geared toward students working to overcome inequity in our school systems. Idealist (www.idealist.org) can help you find places to volunteer (search under organizations and enter "education" as a keyword).

JOIN YOUR LOCAL SCHOOL BOARD. The school board sets the vision for the school district, prioritizes allocations of funds, and makes a huge difference for the schools in your community. The National School Boards Association (www.nsba.org) has information on how to run—or if you don't wish to, how to attend meetings.

VOLUNTEER AT YOUR LOCAL PUBLIC SCHOOL. Under the Trump Administration, public school budgets are likely to be stretched even further than they already are. Volunteer your time with an after-school program to help at-risk youth, or coach a sports team. Money can go a long way to improving education, but nothing helps children more than having a genuine friend and mentor.

BECOME A TEACHER. In an era of shrinking education budgets, quality teachers are harder to come by than ever before. The future of our country begins in the classroom, and becoming a teacher can make an immediate and lifelong change in students' lives. (And if you can't become a teacher, tell one how much you appreciate what she or he does: it's a tough job, and without teachers, there is no education.)

CONTACT YOUR REPRESENTATIVES. Tell local, state, and federal politicians your position on education reform and make sure that they're accountable on pending bills. If they fail to take a constructive position, call and let them know. And if they take an action that you support, let them know that too. There's strength in numbers, so tell your friends to do the same.

SIGN PETITIONS. Petitions can create change by letting lawmakers know how their constituents feel. Sign them online and off. Create your own (www.change.org) or volunteer to help sign up others for the pen-and-paper kind. After you sign, don't forget to pass them along.

DEPLOY SOCIAL MEDIA. If you care about education, let as many people as possible know. Share important education news and, of course, your opinions.

BOOKS TO READ

Democratic Ethical Educational Leadership: Reclaiming School Reform by Steven Jay Gross and Joan Poliner Shapiro (Routledge, 2015). A discussion of the "New DEEL" (acronym from the title), organized around five leadership principles to integrate democracy, social justice, and school reforms to reclaim school reform.

Reign of Error: The Hoax of the Privatization Movement and the Danger to America's Public Schools by Diane Ravitch (Vintage, 2014). An argument that American education is not in a crisis but faces a concerted effort to destroy public schools.

Savage Inequalities: Children in America's Schools by Jonathan Kozol (Broadway Books, 2012). A look at the educational inequalities that mirror the wealth inequalities of this country.

"You know if you shoot an eagle, kill an eagle, they want to put you in jail for five years. Yet the windmills are killing hundreds and hundreds of eagles. One of the most beautiful, one of the most treasured birds— and they're killing them by the hundreds and nothing happens. So wind is, you know, it is a problem. Plus it's very, very expensive and doesn't work without subsidy. . . . Despite that, I'm into all types of energy."

—Donald Trump[1]

ENERGY

THE BACKGROUND

When our country was founded, fuel consisted primarily of wood and water—combined with human effort to collect it and direct it. Wood fed the fires that warmed people's homes. It also built the dams and structures that turned water into energy at the grain and lumber mills supporting American industry. And as the steam engine began its rise in the early 1800s, wood initially provided its power.

However, during the nineteenth century, coal slowly became the fuel of choice as it was more efficient and simpler to transport. Steam-powered mills, much easier to situate without the need for proximity to water, proliferated, as did steam-powered boats. Soon the locomotive and its growing network of tracks pushed America's population, industry, and energy consumption into every corner of the rapidly expanding country. By the end of the 1800s, coal, primarily from Pennsylvania, Ohio, and West Virginia, was powering America.

The second half of the nineteenth century saw the ascent of oil, refined mainly for use as kerosene for lighting, but by century's end it was also used to power the internal combustion engine. Its growing popularity increased the fortunes of John D. Rockefeller, one of the wealthiest people in American history, whose Standard Oil controlled 90 percent of the United States' oil supply in 1899.

Meanwhile, in 1879, Thomas Edison's invention of a reliable light bulb helped introduce electricity to American homes. Edison's company, Edison General Electric Company (now known more familiarly as General Electric), along with those of his competitors, grew rapidly, and by the 1930s regulated electric utilities, most using coal-powered steam plants, were bringing electricity to much of America. Soon, President Franklin D. Roosevelt's monumental Tennessee Valley Authority and Rural Electrification Administration projects brought power to the communities that had been without.

Throughout the first half of the twentieth century, America's industrial output grew rapidly, and the country became increasingly enamored with the lifestyle that abundant energy provided. The explosive growth of the automobile meant another boom for oil, while the continued expansion of electricity into every aspect of American life expanded the demand for coal. Natural gas, which had been used primarily for lighting in the 1800s, also became a source of heating. Fossil fuel use reached a crescendo with World War II and the prosperity and development that followed.

But economic growth soon exposed two significant (and ongoing) challenges to America's appetite for energy. The first was energy's environmental impact. The postwar record heights of energy consumption, coupled with increased chemical production, produced air and water pollution so severe it could no longer be ignored. This led to the establishment of the Environmental Protection Agency (EPA), and the passage of the Clean Air Act of 1970 (an improvement over an earlier version) and the Clean Water Act in 1972. All of these measures have successfully reined in energy industry practices—and were put into play under a rather unlikely champion of the environment, President Richard M. Nixon.

The second challenge was America's dependence on foreign energy sources. To answer an ever-increasing demand for fossil fuels, the country began sourcing energy, particularly oil, from overseas. In 1973, gasoline prices skyrocketed when the Organization of Petroleum Exporting Countries (OPEC) oil cartel, largely controlled by Arab countries, decided to boycott the United States for its support of Israel. Long lines appeared at gas stations, exposing for the first time the vulnerability underlying America's energy addiction. (A similar crisis in 1979 only heightened this sense of unease.)

Environmental and geopolitical concerns have continued to influence energy policy in the decades since. The popularity of nuclear power—first generated commercially in 1958 and now supplying about 19 percent of the nation's electricity—has grown and waned numerous times as the public weighs high-profile environmental disasters against nuclear's low carbon footprint. Clean energy–producing hydroelectric dams have been dismantled because of their impact on fisheries. Offshore drilling's promise to open vast domestic oil reserves has been offset by disasters like BP's Deepwater Horizon explosion, resulting in the largest oil spill in U.S. history. The fracking revolution in energy extraction has revitalized American fossil fuel independence—but with an environmental cost that has divided communities across the country. Meanwhile, renewable "green" energy sources such as solar and wind power have grown rapidly as technology improves and costs drop—according to the U.S. Energy Information Administration, energy production from wind and solar reached record highs in 2015, accounting for 13.44 percent of domestically produced electricity.

Today, America, still mired in foreign conflicts aimed at protecting our strategic energy interests, grapples with whether the economic benefits of fossil fuels outweigh their resulting environmental damage. Even though these economic benefits primarily reward wealthy investors, many have been convinced it is better to ignore science than to disrupt our economy, especially in its fragile postrecession state. It's an argument that won't be settled soon, especially as Americans constitute less than 5 percent of the world's population but consume 26 percent of the world's energy.

WHAT DID BARACK OBAMA DO?

While Obama often described his energy strategy for America as "all of the above,"[2] perhaps his most important achievement in energy was to align U.S. energy policy with the reality of human-induced climate change.

Beginning with the American Recovery and Reinvestment Act of 2009, Obama allocated more than $90 billion to promote programs that developed new, sustainable energy sources and promoted conservation. Much of his work on energy throughout the rest of his administration was devoted to these two areas.

To promote sustainable energy, in 2015 Obama got Congress to extend the tax investment credit for solar and wind power until 2020. He also made available low-interest loans and grants for development of wind, solar, and other sustainable energies as well as the technologies, such as batteries, that support them.

To promote conservation, Obama offered tax incentives and grants for energy efficiency retrofits for existing homes and buildings. He increased energy efficiency standards in automobiles, trucks, appliances, and building construction. And he allocated funding for clean mass transportation.

Some of Obama's most contentious work on energy work was in environmental impact. Obama's environmental work is covered in the Environment chapter, p. 77, but the initiative that particularly relates to his energy policy is his attempt to use the Clean Air Act to reduce emissions from energy plants, a third of which are coal-powered. His 2015 Clean Power Plan sought to reduce carbon emissions in electrical production by 32 percent by 2030. However, in February 2016, the Supreme Court put the plan on hold pending judicial review, where it remains.

Obama took seriously his stewardship of U.S. government lands (also known as public lands), which comprise 28 percent of the United States' land mass. His effort to protect large tracts of the most environmentally sensitive areas conflicted with the desires of drilling and mining companies, which lease these lands for natural resource extraction. It also affected leases for oil and gas fracking; in 2015, the administration released guidelines requiring disclosure of construction techniques and chemicals used in fracking, as well as tightening safety standards. The response was a legal fight; eventually the U.S. District Court in Wyoming struck down these guidelines.

Not all of Obama's efforts restricted fossil fuel production. For instance, he opened up new areas for offshore oil exploration in the Gulf of Mexico. But it was two factors he had little control over, the drop in consumption caused by the Great Recession and the domestic oil and natural gas boom sparked by fracking, that had some of the largest impacts on U.S. energy policy during his administration.

According to U.S. Energy Information Agency statistics, between 2008 and 2015:

- Production of all forms of energy rose 20 percent.
- Production and consumption of renewable forms of energy increased 34 percent.
- Consumption of energy overall dropped 1.4 percent.

WHAT MIGHT DONALD TRUMP DO?

Though vague and at times contradictory, Donald Trump has been fairly consistent about key points in his energy policy. He has said he would roll back or remove regulations on carbon emissions and government land stewardship. He has threatened to weaken the EPA, which enforces many of these regulations, and he has pledged to withdraw from the global commitments under the Paris Agreement on climate change.

He has also said he would like to roll back or remove any incentives or grants for sustainable energy, which he has called "really just an expensive way of making the tree huggers feel good about themselves."[3]

The people he has chosen to advise him in his post-election transition support these views. Marc Short, former president of Freedom Partners, the political donor group of the Koch brothers (whose family made its eleven-figure fortune refining crude oil into gasoline) is now a senior advisor. Michael McKenna, a lobbyist for Koch Industries, is Trump's key advisor on the Department of Energy. Trump's energy transition team is headed by Michael Catanzaro, another lobbyist for Koch Industries and fracking giant Devon Energy Corp. Trump's leading candidate for Secretary of Energy is fracking billionaire and outspoken EPA critic Harold Hamm.

Another inside-the-beltway fossil fuel enthusiast tapped

by Trump to head the EPA transition is Myron Ebell, a climate change denier who directs the Competitive Enterprise Institute, a Washington think tank funded by ExxonMobil—and Koch Industries.

WHAT YOU CAN DO

CONSERVE ENERGY. This is a simple and very direct way of keeping money out of the hands of the people driving Trump's destructive energy agenda. The National Wildlife Federation offers helpful tips on how you can do it (www.nwf.org).

A more personal way to conserve energy is to assess your carbon footprint and try to lower it through lifestyle changes. The Nature Conservancy in partnership with UC Berkeley has a great carbon footprint calculator (www.nature.org/greenliving/carboncalculator).

SPEND YOUR ENERGY DOLLARS WISELY. It's impossible not to consume some form of energy, but the way we spend energy dollars can help shift energy policy. Most electrical utilities offer options for buying power generated via sustainable sources, such as wind and solar. They may cost more, but doing so shifts your usage away from coal and other fossil fuels by supporting the utilities' investment in renewables. The Department of Energy has a list showing programs available in many states (www.energy.gov).

If you need to buy gasoline, the company you choose sends a message as well. The "green living" website Earth's Friends offers a frank assessment of the best and worst oil companies in terms of environmental impact (www.earthsfriends.com /environmental-gas-station).

SUPPORT AND/OR JOIN ORGANIZATIONS FIGHTING FOR SUSTAINABLE ENERGY AND AGAINST THE EXCESSES OF FOSSIL FUELS. The Natural Resources Defense Council, like so many organizations leading the effort for progressive energy policies, is best known for its environmental work, but it has strong programs advocating sustainable energy and fights against the growth of fossil fuel and nuclear power (www.nrdc.org).

The Union of Concerned Scientists is a U.S.-based nonprofit scientific organization founded in 1969 at the Massachusetts Institute of Technology. It uses science to help the public understand some of the most crucial issues facing the world, including arms proliferation, the risks of nuclear power, and climate change. Its efforts on behalf of sustainable energy are invaluable (www.ucsusa.org).

The Sierra Club's Beyond Fossil Fuels Project puts the considerable experience of the well-known environmental group, founded in 1892 by John Muir, behind energy activism. It is now extremely adept at influencing legislation by advocating for clean energy while litigating against

coal, oil, and natural gas (www.sierraclub.org/beyond-fossil
-fuels).

Greenpeace's End Oil and Gas Project also puts a powerful
environmental group behind efforts against fossil fuels, but
Greenpeace uses direct action—often spectacular, photo-op-
generating acts of protest—as a central part of its work (www
.greenpeace.org).

BOOKS TO READ

*The Great Transition: Shifting from Fossil Fuels to Solar and Wind
Energy* by Lester R. Brown, Emily Adams, Janet Larsen,
and J. Matthew Roney (Norton, 2015). How the old
energy economy—that of oil, natural gas, and coal—
is being replaced by one based on new sources of energy.
*The Grid: The Fraying Wires Between Americans and Our Energy
Future* by Gretchen Bakke, Ph.D. (Bloomsbury USA,
2016). A history of America's electrical grid and its need
for repair, how it is impeding progress for newer energy
sources, and ways it is being reimagined for the future.
*Power from the People: How to Organize, Finance, and Launch Local
Energy Projects* by Greg Pahl (Chelsea Green Publishing,
2012). A guide to organizing, financing, and launching
projects to move from centralized power to local power in
a time of peak oil and climate change.

The Power Surge: Energy, Opportunity, and the Battle for America's Future by Michael Levi (Oxford University Press, 2013). The battle over energy revolutions—oil and gas versus new energy sources—how both see their future in American economics, security, and safety, and how to find a combined way forward to improve our way of life.

"I'm not going to cut Social Security like every other Republican and I'm not going to cut Medicare or Medicaid. Every other Republican is going to cut, and even if they wouldn't, they don't know what to do because they don't know where the money is. I do."

—Donald Trump[1]

ENTITLEMENT PROGRAMS

THE BACKGROUND

In 1935, during the depths of the Great Depression, nearly 20 percent of the American labor force was unemployed. The urban homeless banded together in ramshackle settlements nicknamed Hoovervilles, sleeping under cardboard boxes and filthy tents. In the rural West, drought-induced dust storms forced tens of thousands of Americans to abandon their farms. There were few government programs in place to help the needy, so the jobless depended on soup kitchens, charity, and the withering hope that life would one day get better.

President Franklin D. Roosevelt was elected into office in 1932 with a mandate to put America back to work. His famous New Deal consisted of the "3 Rs": Relief, Recovery, and Reform. Chief among the New Deal programs was the Works Progress Administration, which at its peak employed 8.5 million workers to carry out infrastructure projects. Other programs, such as the Tennessee Valley Authority, improved farming efficiency and brought electricity to remote regions of the South. Thanks to New Deal programs, unemployment steadily decreased among working-age people.

But while the able-bodied could finally put food on the table thanks to government employment, poverty rates among seniors exceeded 50 percent. Most elderly Americans could not work, and the stock market crash of 1929 had destroyed what little savings they had accumulated. Roosevelt knew that it was the duty of government to help them. "No greater tragedy exists in modern civilization than the aged, worn-out worker who after a life of ceaseless effort and useful productivity must look forward for his declining years to a poorhouse," he said that same year. "A modern social consciousness demands a more humane and efficient arrangement."[2]

Roosevelt fulfilled his promise in 1935 by signing the Social Security Act, which guaranteed a small but vital monthly benefit to seniors. To fund it, Congress created the Social Security trust fund, financed by employees' paychecks. The first official Social Security card was mailed to John David Sweeney Jr., the twenty-three-year-old scion of a wealthy factory owner, and a Republican. The Social Security tax was implemented in 1937, and the first payment, check no. 00-000-001 for $22.54, was issued to Ida May Fuller of Ludlow, Vermont, on January 31, 1940. (Fuller died at age 100 after collecting $22,888.92.)

By 1960, the poverty rate among seniors had fallen dramatically. By 1995, it was below 10 percent. Today the program remains a critical lifeline, with more than sixty million people drawing Social Security benefits. Sixty-one percent of seniors depend on Social Security for the majority of their income, and without it more than 40 percent of seniors would fall into poverty. The program has become so engrained in society that it's called the "third rail of American politics." Touch it, and you're toast. Barry Goldwater, the Republican presidential nominee in 1964, learned this the hard way: After running on a platform of making Social Security optional, among other extreme proposals, he lost by nearly sixteen million votes to Lyndon B. Johnson (and by nearly 20 percentage points among seniors).

The retirement age for Social Security has gradually increased to sixty-seven, and conservative legislators have made attempts to decrease the annual rate at which benefits increase, known as the cost-of-living adjustment. In 2005, George W. Bush attempted a "partial privatization" of Social Security, a longtime dream of Republicans that would allow people to divert portions of their Social Security withholdings into privately managed accounts. His proposal died after critics warned that privatization represented a giveaway for wealth managers and could destroy retirees' savings during a recession.

Franklin Roosevelt had envisioned Social Security as a "comprehensive package of protection" against the "hazards and vicissitudes of life." But it didn't go as far as he had hoped. Among the hazards and vicissitudes left out of the law was medical care. An original provision of the Social Security Act also guaranteed medical care for seniors, but it was removed out of fears it would kill the bill. This task would not be fulfilled until the election of President Johnson.

Promising a sweeping series of anti-poverty programs collectively known as the Great Society, Johnson entered his term with the most significant social-reform mandate since Franklin Roosevelt. By 1965, barely half of Americans over sixty-five had health insurance, and those who did were paying much higher rates than the young due to increased risk. Even with Social Security benefits, 35 percent of the elderly were still living in poverty, largely due to unaffordable health care costs.

Johnson's solution was to expand Social Security to include universal medical coverage for seniors. "No longer will older Americans be denied the healing miracle of modern medicine," Johnson declared in 1965. The program Congress subsequently created, which became known as Medicare, guaranteed basic health insurance for all Americans over age sixty-five, regardless of income or preexisting health conditions. By the 1980s the poverty rate among the elderly had fallen to 15 percent, largely due to Medicare. In 2003, led by the George W. Bush Administration, Congress expanded Medicare to subsidize prescription drugs, creating a program known as Medicare Part D.

In addition to creating Medicare, Congress also established Medicaid, a social health care program for the poor. Unlike Medicare, Medicaid only covers individuals and families with limited income. Also unlike Medicare, which is administered by the federal government, Medicaid provides states with broad leeway to determine eligibility and implementation. In conjunction with other Great Society programs under Johnson, Medicaid helped bring the overall poverty rate from 19 percent in 1964 to 11.2 percent within ten years. It has stayed below 16 percent nationally ever since. Medicaid now provides health coverage for more than seventy million low-income Americans. According to the Congressional Budget Office, during any given month Medicaid serves thirty-three million children, twenty-seven million adults, six million seniors, and ten million disabled people.

While Medicaid is funded jointly by the federal government and the states, Social Security and Medicare are funded by your payroll taxes under the Federal Insurance Contributions Act (FICA). The FICA tax is split evenly between employees and employers. Currently, employees' share of Social Security and Medicare taxes are 6.2 percent and 1.45 percent, respectively.

WHAT DID BARACK OBAMA DO?

Social Security did not change under President Obama, although he called for expanding benefits late in his second term. "We should be strengthening Social Security," he said in a speech in Elkhard, Indiana. "And not only do we need to strengthen its long-term health, it's time we finally made Social Security more generous, and increased its benefits so that today's retirees and future generations get the dignified retirement that they've earned."[3]

This was a pivot. In 2012, when attempting to forge a "grand bargain" on fiscal policy with Republican House Speaker John Boehner, Obama suggested cuts to Social Security by using a less-generous formula for how the cost-of-living adjustment is calculated. The president quickly backed off this proposal after progressive uproar led by Senator Bernie Sanders of Vermont.

The Social Security trust fund is solvent today, but problems loom. Baby boomers are retiring so quickly—10,000 people per day—that the trust fund is expected to run out by 2034, at which point recipients may only receive 79 percent of their benefits. Many Republicans cite this as proof that Social Security is broken, but relatively simple fixes such as raising the Social Security income tax cap so the wealthy pay more into the system, or limiting benefits for the well-off, can make the program solvent for at least another seventy-five years.

House Speaker Paul Ryan has claimed that under Obama, "Medicare is going broke." This is not true. According to the *Washington Post*, "The Affordable Care Act actually strengthened the near-term outlook of the [Medicare] Part A trust fund" by raising "an additional $63 billion for the Part A trust fund between 2010 and 2019."[4] However, the Medicare trust fund, which mainly covers hospital stays and hospice care, *is* in danger of depleting by 2028, at which point the fund could cover only 87 percent of expenses. Like Social Security's trust fund, the Medicare trust fund can be made solvent by raising payroll taxes, asking wealthy recipients to pay slightly more, or allowing the government to negotiate better deals with pharmaceutical companies.

Under Obama, Medicaid has grown dramatically. For states that expanded Medicaid under the Affordable Care Act, Obama increased the Medicaid eligibility threshold to 133 percent of the poverty line. This change has allowed an estimated 15.7 million people to gain health coverage. For more information on the Affordable Care Act, see the chapter on Obamacare, p. 135.)

WHAT MIGHT DONALD TRUMP DO?

Trump has sent dramatically mixed signals on his plans for Social Security, Medicare, and Medicaid. Regarding Social Security, Trump has said, "We're not going to hurt the people who have been paying into Social Security their whole life."[5] During a Republican debate, Trump stated, "It is my intention to leave Social Security as it is."[6] But as the Associated Press reported, the man heading the Trump transition team's Social Security effort is Michael Korbey, "a former lobbyist who has spent much of his career advocating for cutting and privatizing the program." Korbey has called Social Security "a failed system, broken and bankrupt," and he was a key advocate for George W. Bush's failed privatization bid.[7] Another member of Trump's transition team, Tom Leppert, put forth a plan for partially privatizing the program when he ran for a Senate seat in Texas in 2012.

Under Trump and a Republican-controlled Congress, the GOP will likely make another go at partial or complete privatization of Social Security. When House Speaker Paul Ryan took control of the House Budget Committee in 2011, he also proposed $1.2 trillion in Social Security cuts as well as a proposal to partially privatize the program. While privatization could result in higher returns for Americans during a booming economy, a recession could do major damage. For example, the Center for American Progress estimates that "A person with a private Social Security account similar to what President George W. Bush proposed in 2005 that was invested in stocks retiring on October 1, 2008, after saving for thirty-five years (since 1973), would have seen a negative return on their account—an effective −0.6 percent net annual real rate of return—and lost $26,000 on the market."[8] Because the traditional Social Security trust fund is invested in the safest possible vehicle—nonnegotiable U.S. Treasury bonds—returns are limited, but losses are close to impossible.

For a time, Trump promised that he would not touch Medicare; nevertheless, Trump's presidential transition website says he will "modernize Medicare."[9] What does "modernize" mean? If you ask Paul Ryan, it means transforming traditional single-payer Medicare into a "premium support" or "voucher" system. Instead of the federal government paying for hospital stays, doctor appointments, prescription drugs, and other vital services, seniors would simply receive a subsidy with which they could purchase private insurance. As Paul Waldman wrote in the *Washington Post,* "If you can't afford any of the available plans with what the voucher is worth, tough luck. The whole point is to transfer the expense from Medicare to the seniors themselves."[10] A Kaiser Family Foundation analysis of Mitt Romney and Paul Ryan's Medicare plan from 2012 concluded that it would result in higher premiums for 59 percent of Medicare recipients—in some cases hundreds of dollars per month more.

Trump has also said he wouldn't "touch" Medicaid, but his presidential transition page vows to "maximize flexibility for States in administering Medicaid, to enable States to experiment with innovative methods to deliver healthcare to our low-income citizens."[11] Though it is extremely vague,

Trump's language likely alludes to Paul Ryan's plan to transform Medicaid into a block grant program. Currently, states receive matching federal funds for Medicaid based on a complicated formula that takes into account patient need. Under Ryan's plan, the federal government would provide a fixed amount of money to states. Republicans have long been in favor of block grants. "Y'all would save a lot of money if you let us run the program," then-Mississippi governor Haley Barbour told a congressional committee in 2011.[12] The federal government would indeed save money—nearly $1 trillion over a decade according a recent Republican plan— but at the expense of the most vulnerable Americans. After reviewing Paul Ryan's Medicaid plan from 2012, the Urban Institute estimated that it would lead states to drop between 14.3 million and 20.5 million people from Medicaid within ten years.

WHAT YOU CAN DO

JOIN OR DONATE TO THE AARP. If you are fifty years old or over, you can join the American Association of Retired Persons. With thirty-eight million members, the AARP is one of the most powerful lobbying group in the United States, spending more than $7 million each year lobbying the federal government to ensure that Social Security and Medicare benefits are not cut.

The AARP vehemently opposed George W. Bush's attempts to partially privatize Social Security. After the group spent extensively on an advertising campaign against Bush's proposal, five Republican senators abandoned their support of the plan, and the administration soon gave up. More than 20 percent of Medicaid dollars are spent on poor seniors, and the AARP has opposed all GOP proposals to turn Medicaid into a block grant program.

DONATE TO SOCIAL SECURITY WORKS, a nonprofit organization devoted to protecting and improving the economic security of disadvantaged and at-risk populations by safeguarding the future of Social Security (www.socialsecurityworks.org).

SIGN UP FOR KAISER FAMILY FOUNDATION UPDATES. Kaiser is a nonprofit that focuses on major health issues facing Americans. It offers excellent analysis of proposed government plans and should be your first resource to understand how Donald Trump's healthcare policies will affect current and future retirees (http://kff.org/email).

HELP EDUCATE SENIORS. Seniors represent an enormous voting bloc. Seventy percent of seniors voted in the 2012 election. They are especially likely to vote in midterm elections. In 2010, 61 percent of adults over age sixty-five voted, compared to 21 percent of adults between eighteen and twenty-four. While many seniors are following these issues very closely, if Donald Trump ever plans to cut Social Security, Medicare, or Medicaid, make sure that the seniors in your life are aware of current events. Internet access is not as ubiquitous among the elderly, so face-to-face conversations can be crucial. Organize trips to assisted-living facilities to help spread awareness.

CALL AND WRITE YOUR REPRESENTATIVE. Overwhelming public opposition to George W. Bush's Social Security privatization plan helped frighten lawmakers into changing their votes. Let your elected representatives know that you disapprove of Trump and of the GOP's plan to cut benefits for current and future retirees (https://www.usa.gov/elected-officials).

BOOKS TO READ

False Alarm: Why The Greatest Threat to Social Security and Medicare is the Campaign to "Save" Them by Joseph White (Johns Hopkins University Press, 2001). Why reforms to entitlement programs are getting it wrong.

The Political Life of Medicare by Jonathan Oberlander (University of Chicago Press, 2003). A history of Medicare, its politics and policies, and the future surrounding healthcare politics, aging, and the welfare state.

Social Security Works!: Why Social Security isn't Going Broke and How Expanding It Will Help Us All by Nancy Altman, Eric Kingson (The New Press, 2015). The issues with and benefits of saving Social Security and how it can help resolve growing levels of wealth inequality.

"The concept of global warming was created by and for the Chinese in order to make U.S. manufacturing non-competitive."

—@realDonaldTrump [1]

THE ENVIRONMENT

THE BACKGROUND

The late 1800s was a time of urban wonders, with gleaming machines and tremendous factories producing goods at an efficiency never before thought possible. But given that conditions at these factories were often unsanitary, squalid, and dangerous, progressive reformers were hard at work trying to improve them. However, many other progressives—especially President Theodore Roosevelt —realized that the countryside needed attention as well, and the notion of conservation in America was born.

The first wave of conservation rose in reaction to what Roosevelt saw was an overexploitation of natural resources. An avid hunter, he was dismayed when the bison population, once estimated to be in the tens of millions, had dwindled down to three hundred. This coincided with the eradication of elk and bighorn sheep, along with mass deforestation. Roosevelt later wrote, "We have become great because of the lavish use of our resources. But the time has come to inquire seriously what will happen when our forests are gone, when the coal, the iron, the oil, and the gas are exhausted, when the soils have still further impoverished and washed into the streams, polluting the rivers, denuding the fields and obstructing navigation."

After becoming president in 1901, Roosevelt created the United States Forest Service and established 150 national forests, 51 federal bird reserves, 4 national game preserves, and 5 national parks. In a country that was expanding at a ferocious pace, generating vast sums of wealth and outdoing itself every year with new inventions, Roosevelt set aside 230 million acres of public land as a sanctuary from the forces of modernity.

Then, in the summer of 1931, the rain stopped. In the Midwest, crops withered and died, and the winds drew in the naked topsoil softened by relentless plowing, spawning dust storms that spread beyond 100 million acres. The Dust Bowl, as it became known, was the worst environmental disaster in the history of the United States. To prevent another such catastrophe, environmentalism during the societal reforms of the New Deal turned more practical, providing incentives for farmers to rotate their crops, turn more land into pasture, and apply other methods to prevent soil erosion. By 1938, dust storms were down 65 percent.

While entire forests could be saved with a stroke of a pen, and farmers taught better land use techniques, later environmental issues posed more complicated threats. During the 1950s and '60s, chemical companies dumped toxic waste in a neighborhood within Niagara Falls, New York, known as Love Canal, resulting in high incidences of leukemia. Not long after, the Three Mile Island nuclear power plant in Dauphin County, Pennsylvania, nearly melted down, causing the release of radioactive gases. Around the country, sulfur dioxide from coal-fired power plants triggered acid rain, corroding steel structures and causing catastrophic damage to plants and animals. Chlorofluorocarbons (CFCs) released from cooling units were burning holes in the ozone layer, a natural shield in the stratosphere that absorbs most of the sun's ultraviolet radiation. Americans were realizing that the consequences of poor environmental stewardship were no longer local.

The Clean Air Act, passed in 1963, was the first in a series of laws designed to curb widespread air pollution. Later administered by the Environmental Protection Agency (EPA), created by Richard M. Nixon in 1970 (see the Energy chapter, page 49), air-pollution laws reduced emissions of six common pollutants—particles, ozone (a ground-level pollutant, different from the ozone layer), lead, carbon monoxide, nitrogen dioxide, and sulfur dioxide—by 69 percent between 1970 and 2014. Meanwhile, the Endangered Species Act of 1973 helped protect hundreds of species nearing extinction. In 1987, dozens of nations came together under the Montreal Protocol and agreed to phase out CFCs and other ozone-depleting substances. The treaty was ultimately ratified by 197 countries and ozone holes have since shrunk dramatically.

Today we face a far more existential threat, though its symptoms are often invisible. By burning fossil fuels and destroying forests, swamps, and grasslands, we release carbon dioxide (CO_2) into the atmosphere, approximately half of which lingers and causes a warming "greenhouse effect." This process causes glaciers to melt and sea levels to rise, eventually deluging coastal communities. Climate change also means more tumultuous, unpredictable weather.

Ninety-seven percent of climate scientists concur that the world faces dire consequences if we don't decrease the release of CO_2. (Their research also demonstrates that it is humans who are responsible for this rapidly warming climate.) As President Obama said in 2015, climate change will lead to "submerged countries. Abandoned cities. Fields that no longer grow. Political disruptions that trigger new conflict, and even more floods of desperate peoples seeking the sanctuary of nations not their own."[2]

WHAT DID BARACK OBAMA DO?

Among President Obama's most notable failed initiatives was the American Clean Energy and Security Act, which would have set a limit on the total amount of greenhouse gases that can be released nationally and allowed companies to buy and sell emission permits. Cap and trade, as it was known, narrowly passed in the U.S. House of Representatives in 2009 but ultimately died in the Senate. Despite this failure, Obama managed to leave behind a strong environmental legacy largely through executive actions. His accomplishments include:

- Signing the Paris Agreement, a nonbinding international collaborative action plan designed to avoid the worst impacts of climate change. More than one hundred countries have announced their support for taking measures to limit global warming to 1.5 degrees Celsius.
- Authorizing the Clean Power Plan, which aims to reduce carbon dioxide emissions from electrical power plants by 32 percent (relative to 2005 levels) within twenty-five years. Although not as comprehensive as the 2009 cap-and-trade bill, the Clean Power Plan allowed Obama to bypass

Congress and order power plants to reduce emissions.

- Updating the Corporate Average Fuel Economy standards. In 2011, Obama announced an agreement with the thirteen largest automakers to increase fleet-wide fuel efficiency standards from 25 miles per gallon (MPG) to 54.5 MPG by model year 2025. These new standards will cut greenhouse gas emissions from cars and light trucks in half by 2025.
- Banning offshore Arctic oil drilling through 2022. Burning the oil from the Arctic would contribute to climate change, and if any spills occurred they would be nearly impossible to clean up due to the harsh climate.
- Designating nineteen new national monuments, including 240,000 acres of wildlife habitat in New Mexico. By the end of his presidency, Obama had protected more land and water—more than 265 million acres—than any other president.

WHAT MIGHT DONALD TRUMP DO?

In 2015, Trump told Fox News, "Environmental Protection, what they do is a disgrace and every week they come out with new regulations. . . . We'll be fine with the environment. We can leave a little bit, but you can't destroy businesses."[3] During the Republican primary debates, Trump threatened to dismantle the EPA: "We are going to get rid of it in almost every form. We're going to have little tidbits left but we're going to take a tremendous amount out."[4]

While Trump has wavered on many issues, he has remained remarkably consistent on the environment. He has already tapped Myron Ebell, a leading climate change skeptic, to lead his EPA transition team, a man who bragged to Congress that he was featured in a Greenpeace "Field Guide to Climate Criminals." He told *Vanity Fair* in 2007, "There has been a little bit of warming . . . but it's been very modest and well within the range for natural variability, and whether it's caused by human beings or not, it's nothing to worry about."[5]

Trump has also vowed to pull out of the Paris Agreement, which he can easily accomplish. He has promised to repeal regulations to bring back coal mining—one of the dirtiest power sources—but it's doubtful he can, since the fracking boom has led to a glut of cheap natural gas. Even so, Trump can easily thwart Obama's pledge to cut U.S. carbon emissions up to 28 percent by 2025 from 2005 levels. As of this writing, the Clean Power Plan is at the center of major litigation, and a ruling is expected in early 2017. Even if the court affirms the plan's legality, Trump has many ways he could weaken or dismantle it.

Even without Trump, the Republican Congress has an anti-environmental agenda ready to go. Over the years Republicans have proposed cutting EPA funding by a third, slashing funding for renewable energy by half, repealing coal regulations, fast-tracking oil and gas drilling permits on federal land, banning funds to create or expand wildlife refuges, chopping budgets for repairing the country's aging sewage systems, and blocking the EPA from enforcing rules limiting exposure to lead paint, among other proposals.

While Trump can weaken many Obama administration regulations, there are limits to what he can do. He cannot unilaterally abolish the EPA—only Congress can. Furthermore, presidents usually have difficulty repealing their predecessors' regulations. As Jody Freeman of the Harvard Law School Environmental Law Program points out, "History suggests that while new administrations make a grand show of reviewing their predecessor's rules—looking particularly closely at those still pending, or those rushed through at the last minute—they rescind very few." [6]

Any proposed rule changes would require a notice and comment process, which can last as long as two years and would be subject to lawsuits (which many environmental organizations have pledged to bring). For example, the Bush administration was mired in court for years while attempting to weaken Clinton-era regulations that protected 58.5 million acres of national forests and grasslands from road construction. In short, most of Trump's drastic plans, if he chooses to implement them, will not be easy to accomplish.

WHAT YOU CAN DO

JOIN AN ORGANIZATION. When you lack power, sometimes the next best tactic is to delay. Trump's plans to repeal EPA regulations can be fought and held up in court for years. Many of the following organizations have pledged to fight Trump by any legal means necessary. Contact them or visit their websites to find out how you can support their efforts.

The National Resources Defense Council (NRDC). The NRDC has 2.4 million members and a staff of five hundred lawyers devoted to protecting the environment and will likely lead the vanguard against any anti-environmental agenda. "If the Trump administration follows through on promises made to unravel climate and clean energy efforts, groups like NRDC will use all the tools in our toolkit to fight off federal rollback," Kit Kennedy, director of the energy and transportation program at NRDC, told ThinkProgress after the election (www.nrdc.org).

350. 350 is a global climate movement that uses online campaigns, grassroots organizations, and coordinated mass public actions to hold leaders accountable and create climate change solutions (www.350.org).

League of Conservation Voters (LCV). The LCV advocates

for sound environmental laws and policies, holds elected officials accountable for their votes and actions, and elects pro-environment candidates. The League also helps keep members aware of important pending environmental policies so they can contact their lawmakers (www.lcv.org).

Earthjustice. As the country's original and largest non-profit environmental law organization, Earthjustice leverages expertise and commitment to fight for justice and advance the promise of a healthy world for all (www.earthjustice.org).

Audubon Society. Audubon's mission is to conserve and restore natural ecosystems, focusing on birds, other wildlife, and their habitats for the benefit of humanity and the earth's biological diversity. The society has a national office and regional offices around the country where you can become engaged locally (www.audubon.org).

Sierra Club. The Sierra Club is a national nonprofit with regional offices around the country dedicated to protecting our natural resources through campaigns like Beyond Coal, Beyond Natural Gas, and Get Outdoors. The club has more than 2.4 million members and 20,000 outings each year (www.sierraclub.org).

The Wilderness Society (TWS). The Wilderness Society is a national nonprofit group with offices around the country dedicated to protecting wilderness and inspiring Americans to care for wild places, and has long led the environmental community's efforts to protect places too special to drill (www.wilderness.org).

BlueGreen Alliance. Environmentalism is often positioned as a concern of the elite, ignoring that lower income communities often bear a disproportionate amount of environmental harm. The BlueGreen Alliance unites America's largest labor unions and its most influential environmental organizations to solve today's environmental challenges in ways that create and maintain quality jobs and build a stronger, fairer economy (www.bluegreenalliance.org).

Many states also have effective local grassroots organizations working on environmental issues. In Kentucky, for example, there's Kentuckians for the Commonwealth (www.kftc .org), and in California there's Movement Generation (www .movementgeneration.org).

OTHER IDEAS

VOLUNTEER. Clean up a beach, create a hiking trail, or stuff some envelopes, to find community and help create positive change. Idealist (www.idealist.org) has a good general search engine, while some organizations like the National Park Service (www.nps.gov/getinvolved/volunteer.htm) have a formal volunteer process.

CONTACT YOUR POLITICIANS. It's best to call, write, or email (in that order) your political representatives. Tell them your position on climate change; hold them accountable on bills that are up for review. If they fail to take a position that you're in support of, call and let them know. And if they take an action that you support, let them know that too. There's strength in numbers, so tell your friends to do the same.

SIGN PETITIONS. Petitions can create change by letting lawmakers know that many, many people feel a certain way. Sign them online and off. Create your own (www.change.org) or volunteer to help sign up others for the pen-and-paper kind. And after you sign, don't forget to pass them along.

TAKE A HIKE. If you live in an urban area, it's easy to forget just how beautiful America's countryside is. The more you see of it, the more you'll fight to keep it.

BOOKS TO READ

The Climate Change Playbook: 22 Systems Thinking Games for More Effective Communication about Climate Change by Dennis Meadows, Linda Booth Sweeney, and Gillian Martin Mehers (Chelsea Green Publishing, 2016). Simple, interactive games to help others better understand the causes and consequences of climate change.

This Changes Everything: Capitalism vs. the Climate by Naomi
Klein (Simon and Schuster, 2015). A compelling
argument that climate change is alarmingly real and that
we must make radical changes to reverse course before it's
too late.

Silent Spring by Rachel Carson (Houghton Mifflin, 2002). The
landmark 1962 book about the concern for our future
planet that ignited changes in our laws governing air, land,
and water.

The Sixth Extinction: An Unnatural History by Elizabeth Kolbert
(Picador 2015). How humans have altered the planet and
how we must rethink our existence if we are to continue to
have one.

"When Mexico sends its people, they're not sending their best. They're not sending you. They're not sending you. They're sending people that have lots of problems, and they're bringing those problems with us. They're bringing drugs. They're bringing crime. They're rapists."

—Donald Trump [1]

IMMIGRATION

THE BACKGROUND

Immigration in America can be divided into five eras. The first began when America was still a collection of colonies and witnessed steady migration of Europeans from Northern and Western Europe. These immigrants were tradesmen and small farmers looking for economic opportunity outside of Europe and religious refugees including Quakers, Pilgrims, and French Huguenots who were fleeing persecution. A third class of people, just as important though often overlooked, were the forced laborers. These included indentured servants—essentially slaves who could gain their freedom through work—homeless children, and criminals who were deported as punishment for their crimes. Most hailed from Scotland, Ireland, and England. Even before the widespread exploitation of African slave labor in the eighteenth century, between one-third and one-half of all white immigrants to America were effectively enslaved. A full one-fifth of the early Puritan immigrants were indentured servants. There were even some on the *Mayflower*.

England's Transportation Act (which also populated Australia) sent about 50,000 convicts to the United States between 1717 and 1783—most of them to work as indentured servants. Given the relative expense of white workers (and the annoyance of having to set them free eventually), colonial land owners began taking black slaves from Africa. Between 1525 and 1866, roughly 450,000 Africans were forcibly shipped to the Colonies/United States while the rest of the estimated 12.5 million souls taken as slaves from Africa ended up in South America and the Caribbean—minus the roughly two million who died en route and were thrown into the Atlantic.

America's first immigration laws arrived with the Naturalization Act of 1790, which extended citizenship only to free white people "of good character" who had lived in the country for a minimum of two years. The law was amended in 1795 to extend the residency requirement to five years (a statute still in effect today). The eighteenth century also saw the birth of the first politically motivated immigration bill: the Naturalization Act of 1798, which the Federalists used to try to knock eligible voters out of the Democratic-Republican Party of Thomas Jefferson.

The 1840s brought the second era of our immigration history. Immigrants came to the States fleeing famines in Germany and Ireland as well as the wave of revolutions that swept Europe beginning in 1848. The country also saw its first large-scale Mexican "immigration" when the U.S. annexed Texas in 1845, just prior to the Mexican-American War; suddenly 80,000 Mexicans were living in America without ever having crossed a border. Meanwhile, on the West Coast, Chinese immigrants showed up looking for gold, but ended up, along with the Irish, doing the backbreaking work of building the first intercontinental railroads.

By 1850 there were 2.2 million people living in the United States who had been born in other countries—14.4 percent of the population. A full one-third of the people living in Boston at this time were foreign-born.

The first anti-immigration movement appeared in the 1850s in the form of a party nicknamed the "Know Nothings." This group specifically opposed immigration by Germans and Irish Catholics, who were smeared in the press, denied entry to certain establishments, and generally stigmatized by the rest of society.

The Naturalization Act of 1870 finally gave citizenship to black Americans but stopped short of helping the Asian-born. In fact, the act increased the restrictions on Chinese and Japanese immigrants by making it illegal for them to own land.

The third wave of American immigration began around 1880 as industrialization in Europe created a surplus labor force that fanned out around the world in search of jobs. New technologies like steamships made crossing the Atlantic easier than it had ever been, allowing these workers to come to the United States in droves. In 1892, the Federal government took control of all immigration policing and established Ellis Island in New York Harbor as the main processing center for European immigrants, who mostly hailed from Southern and Eastern Europe. In all, the United States sent back around 2 percent of would-be immigrants for reasons including disease, criminal history, mental illness, or lack of useful work skills. During these years Congress also passed bills prohibiting the immigration of both anarchists and anyone from China.

The fourth era of immigration began with the imposition of tighter immigration restrictions for Europeans, enacted by the Immigration Act of 1924. The act's main distinction was to establish yearly quotas of immigrants from certain countries, with much higher quotas allotted to "desirable" immigrants from Northern and Western Europe and lower quotas set for Southern and Eastern Europeans. This quota system set the tone of immigration policy for the next three decades. When America entered the Great Depression, xenophobia toward foreign-born workers exploded across the country, and lawmakers scrambled to appease their constituents. Congress carried out the first major deportations of Mexican Americans during these years, tossing anywhere from one to two million people back across the border, whether or not they were American citizens. In 1954, the government undertook another mass deportation in the form of "Operation Wetback," which saw suspected illegal immigrants from Mexico hunted down in their homes and places of work by an immigration enforcement squad and forcibly sent back to Mexico.

However, American immigrants did receive some compassion. President Harry Truman looked to Europe after the war and said: "I urge the Congress to turn its attention to this world problem in an effort to find ways whereby we can fulfill our responsibilities to these thousands of homeless and suffering refugees of all faiths." These sentiments gave rise to the Displaced Persons Act in 1948, which allowed another 200,000 Europeans to resettle in the United States. The Immigration and Nationality Act of 1952 finally eliminated race as an entry criteria, but it kept quotas in place for immigrants from everywhere except countries in the Western Hemisphere.

The fifth era of immigration began on a decidedly humane note when President Lyndon B. Johnson signed the Immigration and Nationality Act of 1965. This act did away with the quota system entirely in favor of a visa system. It allowed foreign-born American citizens to sponsor relatives still living in their countries of origin and created preference visa categories for skilled workers. In short, it laid the groundwork for the immigration system we still have today.

The United States now has an annual global limit of

675,000 immigrants, and by 2042 the country's population is expected to be majority nonwhite (i.e., not "of European descent"). However, the newest arrivals won't necessarily have an easy time of it: Due to all the acts and amendments passed over the years, we also have a canon of immigration law that, according to the U.S. Court of Appeals for the Ninth Circuit, is "second only to the Internal Revenue Code in complexity." [2]

WHAT DID BARACK OBAMA DO?

Barack Obama tried to reform immigration policy but was largely thwarted by Congress. On one hand, he acted as a beacon of hope for new immigrants by declaring, for eample, "It is my firm belief that immigration is not something to fear. We don't have to wall ourselves off from those who may not look like us right now, or pray like we do, or have a different last name. Because being an American is about something more than that. What makes us Americans is our shared commitment to an ideal that all of us are created equal, all of us have a chance to make of our lives what we will." [3]

On the other hand, at the end of Obama's presidency eleven million immigrants were still living in the United States illegally, and he was also responsible for repatriating some two million of them during his eight years in office. Depending on how the numbers are crunched, Obama can be considered one of the biggest evictors of immigrants of the last thirty years.

However, in 2014, Obama initiated executive action to delay the deportation of some five million immigrants, including hundreds of thousands of children. Although the actions would not have legalized these people, it would have let such immigrants keep their families together and hold legal employment while Congress worked to reform the immigration code. Ultimately, Obama's actions were blocked by the Supreme Court. Nevertheless, he was able to grant temporary legal status via executive order to 750,000 children whose parents had brought them to the United States from other countries. Referred to collectively as his "Dreamers," these young people are his most direct legacy in terms of immigration reform.

WHAT MIGHT DONALD TRUMP DO?

Throughout his campaign, Donald Trump made many disparaging remarks about immigrants. He has also promised to create a "deportation force"[4] to remove either all of America's estimated eleven million illegal immigrants, or merely the two to three million immigrants he characterizes as "dangerous."[5] Discussing this plan, he actually mentioned the infamous 1954 "Operation Wetback" as his inspiration.[6]

He has proposed completely ceasing immigration from certain countries with large Muslim populations and creating a Muslim registry. Carl Higbie, the head of a Trump-supporting political action committee called Great America, has cited the Japanese internment camps of World War II as a "precedent" for Trump's Muslim registry.[7]

Trump has also pledged to reverse "every unconstitutional executive action"[8] by Obama, which would presumably include his granting of temporary legal status to 750,000 children living in America illegally.

On the other side of the immigration spectrum, entrepreneurs in Silicon Valley are worried that Trump will put restrictions on the H-1B visa program, which they use to bring in much of their overseas talent. According to the National Foundation for American Policy, immigrants have founded more than half of the American-based tech startups valued at $1 billion or more.

And regarding Trump's pledge to construct an "impenetrable, physical, tall, powerful, beautiful"[9] wall between the United States and Mexico, he will need somewhere between $15 billion and $25 billion for its construction. Although he has said that he expects Mexico to pay for the wall, our friends south of the border have flat-out refused to do so.

WHAT YOU CAN DO

DONATE MONEY. The American Civil Liberties Union has already set out an action plan that includes protecting the Dreamers who received presidential protection, resisting any attempt to create a dragnet deportation force a la "Operation Wetback"; preventing "Stop and Frisk" policies from being adopted nationwide; and opposing any ban against Muslims entering the United States or discrimination against Muslims already living here (www.aclu.org).

The American Friends Service Committee is a Quaker organization that both advocates for immigrants at the federal level and works directly with immigrant communities to ensure their rights. Its main goals include demilitarizing the border with Mexico, ensuring all immigrants have the right to work, and ending detention quotas, which require the incarceration of a certain number of immigrants in detention at any given time (www.afsc.org).

The American Immigration Council is a research and analysis group that challenges the misinformation often put out about immigrants in the media and public sphere. Its reports are an important source of facts about immigration that can counter the scapegoating and scaremongering that dominates much of the public discourse on immigrants (www .americanimmigrationcouncil.org).

KNOW YOUR ADVERSARIES. There are three main organizations in Washington pushing for nativist immigration reforms— the Federation for American Immigration Reform, the Center for Immigration Studies, and Numbers USA. If you hear someone mention any of these groups, that is a major red flag that whatever he or she says next is probably highly anti-immigrant.

ORGANIZE AND VOLUNTEER. Trump's campaign capitalized on dividing Americans based on their ethnicities. Consider bringing all the various members of your community together. Volunteer at a soup kitchen or in a mentoring program. Organize interfaith dialogues at your place of worship and others nearby. Coach a sports team. When people are trying to divide other people, one of the most revolutionary things you can do is unite them. Here are some organizations you can volunteer for:

HIAS. Originally founded in 1881 to help Jews fleeing pogroms in Russia and Eastern Europe, HIAS is now dedicated to the protection of refugees from around the world. It is looking for both highly skilled volunteers, such as lawyers and translators, and as well as anyone who can act as English conversation partners with newly arrived refugees who need to practice their language skills (www.hias.org).

Big Brothers and Big Sisters. Mentoring young people is admirable no matter the political climate, but if you live in an area with many recent immigrants, you'll likely find that the Big Brothers and Big Sisters programs in your neighborhood may have a large number of immigrant children because their parents often work long hours. Mentoring them is an immensely rewarding way to work directly with an immigrant community in your own area (www.bbbs.org).

The Council on American Islamic Relations. This group is America's preeminent NGO working with the American Islamic community. It not only works in Washington, D.C., and in the courts, it also provides direct services to facilitate integration and mutual understanding to Islamic communities in America. Volunteering with your local chapter is a great way to support your local Muslim community (www.cair.com).

Border Angels. Most of the organizations involved in direct action with Mexican immigrants are located in the Southwest and California. One such group is Border Angels, which provides food, water, and clothing to newly arrived immigrants in San Diego County and also free Spanish-language immigration services (www.borderangels.org).

IF YOU NEED HELP . . . The American Immigration Lawyers Association is dedicated to ensuring that immigrants get fair treatment before the law. If you are in need of legal services, it can assist you in finding an immigration lawyer in your area (www.aila.org).

STAND UP TO HATRED. If you see someone suffering verbal abuse because he or she is, or appears to be, an immigrant, go and stand with that person to show your willingness to take a side. If you don't feel comfortable with such a confrontation, report the incident on the website of the Anti-Defamation League. It keeps a running database of anti-Semitic, racist, or bigoted incidents (www.adl.org).

BOOKS TO READ

City of Dreams: The 400-Year Epic History of Immigrant New York by Tyler Anbinder (Houghton Mifflin Harcourt, 2016). The story of New York City, a city of immigrants, as the epicenter of foreign-born contributors to politics, art, and culture, and their lasting impact.

A Different Mirror: A History of Multicultural America by Ronald Takaki (Back Bay Books, 2008). The history of the America of non-Anglo peoples—Native Americans, African Americans, Jews, the Irish, Asians, Latinos, and Muslims—and how they are reshaping the country and what it means to be a citizen.

Harvest of Empire: A History of Latinos in America by Juan Gonzalez (Penguin Books, 2011). A history of Latinos in America, featuring stories from pioneers and what led to their journey to a new homeland.

The Land of Open Graves: Living and Dying on the Migrant Trail by Jason De León (Univ. of California Press, 2015). An anthropologist's study of the suffering and death of undocumented migrants in Arizona's Sonoran Desert.

Scapegoats: How Islamophobia Helps Our Enemies and Threatens Our Freedoms by Arsalan Iftikhar (Hot Books, 2016). An international human rights lawyer's tale of the scapegoating of immigrants.

"It's like in golf. A lot of people—I don't want this to sound trivial—but a lot of people are switching to these really long putters, very unattractive. It's weird. You see these great players with these really long putters, because they can't sink three-footers anymore. And, I hate it. I am a traditionalist. I have so many fabulous friends who happen to be gay, but I am a traditionalist."

—Donald Trump[1]

LGBTQ ISSUES

THE BACKGROUND

Being gay in the United States has never been easy. Throughout most of American history, sexual relations between members of the same gender have been considered a so-called crime against nature, i.e., sexual behavior considered to be indecent by society's current standards. (Anal sex was specifically prohibited by an act of Queen Elizabeth I in 1563, and punished for centuries by harsh prison sentences and steep fines.)

In the early years of our nation, several unsuccessful attempts were made to relax laws against gay men—but not in a way that would seem forward thinking today. For example, in 1779 Thomas Jefferson penned a law for Virginia that decreed castration for men who engage in sodomy—which was actually a liberalization of the previous law that mandated the death penalty. (Jefferson's draft was rejected by the Virginia state legislature.)

Still, the percentage of gay Americans then was presumably equivalent to that today, as the threat of death or any other punishment has never served to curtail homosexual activity—it just sent it underground. The country preferred not to think about the issue; it was seldom discussed; the English word *homosexual* didn't even exist until 1868. Yet many famous Americans of the past were rumored to be gay or bisexual, including Ralph Waldo Emerson, Walt Whitman, and James Buchanan, the fifteenth president of the United States. A lifelong bachelor, Buchanan shared a home for several years with William Rufus King, a senator from Alabama. The two were referred to as "Siamese twins" due to their constant companionship—a prominent Democrat, writing to Mrs. James K. Polk, referred to King as "his [Buchanan's] wife."

Few men lived together openly, however. Lesbians were better able to hide their relationships by calling themselves friends, or by engaging in a "Boston marriage," or what was the equivalent of what is now known as a domestic partnership. One of the most notable Boston marriages was that of pioneering women's rights advocate Jane Addams and her "friend," Mary Rozet Smith.

It wasn't until the 1920s that some gay rights organizations began to appear, but none of these early efforts managed to sustain themselves. However, after World War II, a few enduring groups were founded, including the Mattachine Society, formed in 1950 to fight for gay male rights, and the

Daughters of Bilitis, founded in 1955 to advance lesbian civil rights. Yet the 1950s proved to be the most difficult era for gay men and women in the country's history. This period, marked by fear of communism (which produced the McCarthy hearings and the Red Scare), was also marred by harassment and persecution of gays (known as the Lavender Scare), and scores of men and women were forced to resign from their government jobs. Many gay men were also compelled to undergo various types of psychological therapies to change them, including lobotomies and aversion techniques that, in their most brutal form, delivered electric shocks to the genitals whenever the patient experienced a positive response to erotic pictures of men. These efforts did not work, often leaving patients psychologically scarred for life.

However, in the 1960s, as society began to challenge many of its traditional mores, a nascent national gay rights movement emerged. Then, in 1969, police raided the Stonewall Inn, a gay bar in Manhattan's Greenwich Village. Such raids were typical at the time; atypically, these patrons fought back. Gay liberation was born. Slowly, gays came out of the closet and marched onto the streets.

Meanwhile, the country's antisodomy laws began to be struck down until, in 2003, the Supreme Court invalidated all that remained. And, in the 1990s under President Bill Clinton, the prohibition on open homosexuality in the armed forces was addressed with the so-called Don't Ask, Don't Tell policy.

The rule permitted gays to serve in the military—as long as they did not say they were gay. Progress sometimes went backward. In 1996, the Defense of Marriage Act barred the federal government from recognizing same-sex couples in any legal manner.

During the socially conservative administration of George W. Bush, many states also passed laws prohibiting same-sex unions of any kind. But in 2000, Vermont legalized same-sex civil unions, and three years later Massachusetts legalized same-sex marriage. Finally, in 2015, the Supreme Court ruled in *Obergefell v. Hodges* that all state bans on same-sex marriage were unconstitutional. Gay marriage became the law of the land.

However, even as gay men and women were obtaining equal rights, many states passed so-called religious freedom bills that allow individuals and businesses the right to discriminate against anyone based on their religious principles. Twenty-one states have already enacted some form of religious freedom laws, while at least ten others are considering them. Perhaps the most notorious was the one passed by North Carolina governor Pat McCrory known as HB2, that, among other measures, blocked all North Carolina cities from passing any form of nondiscrimination legislation and prohibited transgender individuals from using their appropriate bathroom facility. The law has cost the state more than $700 million in lost business, celebrity concerts, and sports events—and McCrory his job.

Despite all the advances made in the LGBTQ community, many of them can be rolled back—quickly, easily, and effectively.

WHAT DID BARACK OBAMA DO?

During his Illinois senate campaign in 2004, Barack Obama stated that he did not support same-sex marriage. Eight years later, he announced that he did support it—the first president to do so. Like many other politicians, Obama's evolution into a full supporter of gay rights was slow but steady. His many achievements included working with Congress to pass and sign into law the Matthew Shepard Hate Crimes Prevention Act of 2009, extending federal hate-crimes law to include attacks based on the sexual orientation or gender identity of the victim.

Obama also:

- Established a federal task force on bullying within the Department of Health and Human Services (HHS).
- Supported efforts to ban the use of so-called conversion therapy against minors.

- Repealed Don't Ask, Don't Tell, allowing gays and lesbians to serve openly in the armed forces.
- Refused to defend the Defense of Marriage Act's provision designating marriage as only between a man and a woman.
- Signed an executive order prohibiting federal contractors from discriminating against any employee because of sexual orientation or gender identity.
- Engaged with world leaders to advance the rights of LGBTQ persons around the globe.
- Directed the HHS to establish the first national resource center for older LGBTQ individuals.
- Appointed LGBTQ individuals to many important government posts, including Sharon Lubinski, the first lesbian to become a U.S. marshal.

All in all, Obama could claim more positive lesbian, gay, bisexual, and transgender legislation and support than any other president in American history.

WHAT MIGHT DONALD TRUMP DO?

"Ask yourself," Trump said in June of 2016, "who is really the friend of women and the LGBT community: Donald Trump with his actions, or Hillary Clinton with her words?"

Trump has consistently said he is a champion of gay rights. And he has said that he accepts that gay marriage is now the law of the land.

However . . .

Trump has also said he will appoint justices like Antonin Scalia to the Supreme Court. Scalia consistently voted against any and all gay rights.

Trump has pledged to repeal all or parts of the Affordable Care Act, which protects transgender people from discrimination in health care.

Although he once criticized it, Trump has spoken out in favor of North Carolina's HB2 law, mentioned above.

Although he once said that federal law should protect people from discrimination based on sexual orientation, Trump has expressed support for the First Amendment Defense Act, which would protect those who oppose same-sex marriage based on their religious beliefs from legal action by the federal government.

He has already appointed to powerful positions people who oppose gay rights, including Steve Bannon, his chief strategist, whose Breitbart website has published numerous homophobic comments and headlines such as GAY RIGHTS HAVE MADE US DUMBER, IT'S TIME TO GET BACK IN THE CLOSET.

Trump has said that he wants to nullify all of President Obama's "unconstitutional" executive orders, which might include one that bans anti-LGBTQ discrimination by federal contractors.

WHAT YOU CAN DO

JOIN AN ORGANIZATION. There are many dozens of national groups supporting LGBTQ rights, along with state and municipal organizations

Some of the more prominent national ones include:

Campus Pride. An educational organization for LGBTQ students and their allies. The goal is to help make colleges and universities more LGBTQ-friendly. It also identifies the best and worst campuses for LGBTQ youth. You may want to keep away from the University of Dallas, Illinois' Wheaton College, and Bob Jones University—but go Cornell! Go Macalaster! Go Elon! (www.campuspride.org).

GLAAD. Formerly the Gay & Lesbian Alliance Against Defamation, the group had to change its name due to all the acronym-related additions and subtractions in the gay world. Founded in 1985 to protest the sensationalized AIDS coverage by a local New York newspaper, it has grown into a national organization that works with the media on LGBTQ issues (www.glaad.org).

GLSEN. The Gay, Lesbian & Straight Education Network, founded in 1990, aims to stop discrimination, harassment, and bullying based on sexual orientation, gender identity, and gender expression in K-12 schools. Based in New York, the group has built a network of more than 13,000 educators across America and works locally through chapters in twenty-six states (www.glsen.org).

NGLTF. The National LGBTQ Task Force organizes grassroots advocacy movements on LGBTQ issues. Started in 1973, it also stages the National Conference on LGBT Equality: Creating Change, an annual skills-building event with more than 2,000 attendees (www.thetaskforce.org).

Lambda Legal. The Lambda Legal Defense and Education Fund focuses on LGBTQ issues. Founded in 1971, the group has played a major role in many legal cases pertaining to gay rights, including the Supreme Court's 2003 decision that invalidated sodomy laws (www.lambdalegal.org).

PFLAG. Formerly known as the Parents, Families, and Friends of Lesbians and Gays, it is the country's largest organization for people who are united with and wish to help their LGBTQ loved ones. Founded in 1972 by an elementary school teacher and her husband, it now has more than 500 chapters and 200,000 members and supporters across the country (www.pflag.org).

And don't forget: Act Up, The Human Rights Campaign, The National Gay and Lesbian Chamber of Commerce, Truth Wins Out, and so many more.

In addition, most states have at least one organization working on LGBTQ issues, and many have an equality organization that addresses state issues. They are always looking for volunteers. Look them up online or check Wikipedia (https://en.wikipedia.org/wiki/List_of_LGBT_rights_organizations_in_the_United_States).

VOLUNTEER. Search out local groups. If your city has a Gay and Lesbian Center, show up and ask if they need help. They do!

SPEAK OUT LOUDLY AGAINST BULLYING. If you see bullying in your school or your workplace, don't be silent. Say something. Help those who need your help.

SIGN PETITIONS. Petitions can create change. If you live in a large city, don't pass by those people on the street asking for signatures. Sign. Volunteer to help sign up others. At any moment you can find dozens of petitions online that can effect change—if you sign them. Pass along this information to other people via social media.

USE SOCIAL MEDIA. Don't be afraid to speak up. Your Twitter tweet or YouTube video may go viral and be seen or heard by thousands. Be creative, be clever, be supportive.

WRITE YOUR POLITICAL REPRESENTATIVES. Write powerfully. Write often. Write to as many local, state, and federal leaders as you can.

BOYCOTT. YourTango.com published a piece in 2013 on companies (or their chief executives) that don't support gay rights, including Urban Outfitters, the Salvation Army, and Purina. Spend your dollars where your heart is.

DONATE. Every organization will tell you that what they need most is the money to keep going. So give generously, and as though your future depends on it.

MAKE A GAY FRIEND/MAKE A STRAIGHT FRIEND. Reach out to people, no matter what their orientation. Surveys show that the more gays straight people know, the less likely the latter are to dislike the former. Be a pal, make a pal.

BOOKS TO READ

The Gay Revolution: The Story of the Struggle by Lillian Faderman (Simon and Schuster, 2016). Featuring interviews with politicians, military figures, and LGBTQ citizens, the story of the struggle for equal rights.

Stonewall: Breaking Out in the Fight for Gay Rights by Ann Bausum (Speak, 2016). Written as a history for teen readers, an exploration of the fight for equal rights and the gay rights movement.

Love Wins: The Lovers and Lawyers Who Fought the Landmark Case for Marriage Equality by Debbie Cenziper and Jim Obergefell (Morrow, 2016). A chronicle of the participants and the struggle involved in one of the landmark cases of gay rights in U.S. history.

It's Not Over: Getting Beyond Tolerance, Defeating Homophobia, and Winning True Equality by Michelangelo Signorile (Mariner Books, 2016). Stories of LGBTQ Americans fighting for acceptance and equal rights.

"We have to beat the savages . . . we have to increase the laws, because the laws are not working, obviously. All you have to do is take a look what is going on. And they're getting worse. They're chopping, chopping, chopping, and we're worried about water-boarding. I just think it's—I think our priorities are mixed up."

—Donald Trump[1]

NATIONAL SECURITY

THE OVERVIEW

How does America protect itself? The answer was simpler when borders were physical, long before the advent of intercontinental missiles and computer viruses capable of bringing down power grids. During America's first hundred years, the country did its best to stay out of international affairs. When George Washington left office in 1796, he famously advised Congress to avoid foreign entanglements, especially relating to Europe: "Our detached and distant situation invites and enables us to pursue a different course."[2] During the eighteenth and nineteenth centuries, the physical security of the continental United States was rarely at risk from outside invasion. The American Revolution, the War of 1812, and the Civil War were the only wars fought primarily on American soil.

Although the nineteenth century was a time of relative isolation, in 1823 President James Monroe formulated the

Monroe Doctrine, a unilateral declaration that "The American continents . . . are henceforth not to be considered as subjects of future colonization by any European Powers." It was a shot across Europe's bow and served not only to keep European powers out of the New World, but also to establish all of the Americas as the United States' sphere of influence—an important precedent the country would use later when it became interested in the affairs of Latin America.

By the end of the century American isolationism was giving way to "gunboat diplomacy" as the United States injected itself into Cuba's successful revolution against Spain, a conflict that became known as the Spanish–American War. Soon after, the United States supported Panama's separation from Colombia, allowing Americans to construct and control the Panama Canal connecting the Pacific and Atlantic oceans, facilitating maritime trade.

The short era of U.S. interventionism came to an end after a generation of Americans witnessed the horrors of World War I. Leaving Europe to take care of its own matters, Americans spent the Roaring Twenties ignoring the rest of the world and building up its domestic economy. However, the outbreak of World War II in 1939 touched off an intense debate in America about whether to become involved, but that question was settled when Japan bombed Hawaii's Pearl Harbor in 1941, killing 2,403 Americans.

America emerged from the war as the world's predominant superpower, having not only played an important role in beating Axis powers but also displaying its military might through the controversial dropping of the first atomic bombs on Japan. But soon American and European interests collided with those of the U.S.S.R.'s, igniting the Cold War. The development of long-range bombers, and later intercontinental ballistic missiles with nuclear warheads, brought our now-enemies into much closer range, and at a moment's notice. In 1947, the National Security Act reorganized the armed forces and established both the National Security Council and the Central Intelligence Agency (CIA) to contend with the Soviets and the Chinese. The mid-twentieth century saw American intervention in proxy wars with the U.S.S.R. and/or China around the world, including the Korean War, the Vietnam War, and the Soviet–Afghan War, as well as various coup d'états in Latin America.

With the fall of the Soviet Union in 1991, America became the world's sole superpower. For a time, America used this status to forge international consensus on armed conflict. During the first Gulf War, for instance, America fought Iraq alongside a United Nations coalition comprising more than thirty nations.

That began to change when, only days after the terrorist attacks of September 11, 2001, Congress empowered President George W. Bush to take "all necessary and appropriate force" against those responsible for the attacks. Vice President Dick

Cheney later recalled the mind-set at the time: If there was "a one percent chance" that a threat was real, "we have to treat it as a certainty in terms of our response."[3] This mentality spawned the Bush Doctrine, centered on the use of unilateral preemptive strikes as a defense against a perceived immediate threat to the security of the United States. The United States subsequently invaded Afghanistan, which had harbored al-Qaeda, the terrorist group responsible for the 9/11 attacks. Then, in 2003, America invaded Iraq, claiming to have proof that the country possessed weapons of mass destruction (it didn't) and that it had ties to terrorist organizations including al-Qaeda.

Runaway fears about the next terrorist attack spurred unprecedented growth of national security programs and agencies. At least 263 government organizations were created or reorganized after 9/11 to focus on terrorism and security. In 2010, the *Washington Post* counted some 1,271 government organizations and 1,931 private companies comprising roughly 854,000 civil servants, military personnel, and private contractors with top-secret security clearances working on programs related to homeland security, counterterrorism, and intelligence in about 10,000 locations across the country.

By 2010, the U.S. intelligence budget had ballooned to $80 billion—twice the size it was on September 10, 2001—while military spending had doubled. Today, the total of funds spent annually on national security—the military, homeland security, veteran affairs, the nuclear arsenal, and other big-ticket security items—tops $1 trillion. That's roughly the size of the next seven largest military budgets around the world, combined.

Some of the antiterror operations these funds supported were considered to be human rights violations. During the George W. Bush Administration, secret "black site" prisons and military bases across the globe were used for CIA and Special Forces interrogations in which inmates were subjected to an array of painful contortions and severe deprivations—also known as "enhanced interrogation methods"—responsible for at least 100 detainee deaths. The Bush Administration also expanded "extraordinary rendition," the practice of sending terror suspects to other countries for torture with the aim of extracting information. This practice occurred at least 136 times with the cooperation of fifty-four foreign governments. According to the CIA's own inspector general, the frequency and intensity with which interrogators waterboarded suspects—a technique used to simulate drowning—was neither "efficacious nor medically safe."[4]

Like torture, domestic and international mass surveillance by the National Security Agency broadened under George W. Bush. Thanks to various executive orders and the USA Patriot Act, which was passed by Congress in October 2001, the NSA secretly collected phone records from tens of millions of Americans using data provided by AT&T, Verizon, and BellSouth,[5] and the Bush Administration authorized the

NSA to wiretap, without warrants, international phone calls and emails that travel to or from the U.S. The vast scope of surveillance programs under both President Bush and President Obama was revealed by CIA analyst Edward Snowden, who revealed numerous global surveillance programs, many run by the NSA in cooperation with telecommunication companies and European governments.

During the lead-up to the 2008 presidential election, Congress voted to immunize telecom companies for their cooperation with the NSA and expand the government's ability to track domestic communications without obtaining a specific warrant for each case.

WHAT DID BARACK OBAMA DO?

When President Obama assumed office, he immediately increased troop levels in Afghanistan, where the situation had deteriorated substantially. By early 2010, the United States had 94,000 troops there—up from around 34,000—and 92,000 in Iraq. As the situation in Afghanistan improved, Obama gradually reduced troops, although around 8,000 remain today. In accordance with the U.S.–Iraqi Status of Forces Agreement signed by George W. Bush, Obama had removed all combat troops from Iraq by December 2011, although limited operations have resumed to help defend against the threat of the

Islamic State of Iraq and the Levant (ISIL), a Salafi jihadist unrecognized state and militant group responsible for human rights abuses and ethnic cleansing in Northern Iraq and Syria.

In May 2011, the Obama Administration successfully conducted Operation Neptune Spear, a CIA-led raid on Osama bin Laden's compound in Abbottabad, Pakistan. Bin Laden, the leader of al-Qaeda and mastermind of the 9/11 attacks, was killed by American Special Forces.

Closer to home, in 2014, Obama took steps to end the fifty-year standoff between the United States and Cuba. Communist Cuba had become an ally of the Soviet Union during the Cold War, and the United States responded by forbidding all trade and travel to Cuba. This hostile relationship remained after the fall of the U.S.S.R. as Cuban exiles continued to flee to Florida. Hostilities thawed when Obama negotiated a secret deal where the United States rolled back parts of the embargo and Cuba allowed greater freedoms for its people. Travel there is still restricted, but Americans can now relatively easily receive permission to visit.

Also in 2014, Obama took steps to curtail the NSA's power by requiring that analysts receive permission from the Foreign Intelligence Surveillance Court before pulling records from its massive phone records database. In September 2015, Congress passed a law requiring the government to first secure a targeted warrant to obtain any phone metadata from phone companies. While this was a positive step forward, critics point out that it does little to rein in Executive Order 12333, a directive issued by President Ronald Reagan that gives the NSA the authority to capture, retain, and share with other agencies the communications of U.S. citizens that travel or are stored outside U.S. borders. Given that services like Google and Facebook host user data on an array of global servers, this reality means our personal communications on these services, among others, remain susceptible to government snooping.

Obama also reined in the most aggressive forms of Bush Administration torture. In 2009, he signed an executive order closing all CIA detention facilities and directing interrogators from all agencies, including the CIA, to use only techniques approved in the Army Field Manual. The field manual directive was later codified into law. Although the manual bans torture involving sexual humiliation, nudity, burns, electric shocks, waterboarding, and painful stress positions, it grants limited sessions of sensory and sleep deprivation.

After pulling most American troops from Afghanistan and Iraq, Obama expanded the drone strike program put in place by President Bush to kill terror suspects. In Pakistan, Yemen, and Somalia, for instance, Obama has ordered ten times more strikes than Bush. Under both presidencies, among those killed by drones include eight Americans, only one of whom was the intended target of a strike. Obama has successfully fought in court to exclude judicial review of the legality of such attacks.

Obama ended his tenure with an act of diplomacy: In 2015, the United States and Iran agreed on a framework that reduced international economic sanctions against Iran in exchange for Iran ending its pursuit of nuclear weapons. In January 2016, the White House announced that Iran had completed the necessary steps to dismantle its nuclear weapons program. Before the deal, Iran's breakout time—the time it would take for it to gather enough fissile material to build a weapon—was only two to three months. Today, the breakout time is twelve months or more.

WHAT MIGHT DONALD TRUMP DO?

No one knows what Trump's international relations policies might be—in fact, no one knows if he's even interested in international affairs. After the election, the *Washington Post* reported that Trump had actually been avoiding national security briefings.

Trump initially ran on a platform of isolationism. He called the Iraq War "a big, fat mistake"[6] (although he initially expressed support for the invasion during an interview with radio host Howard Stern). In early 2016, he promised to "shake the rust off of America's foreign policy"[7] and stop meddling in the affairs of foreign nations. "We will no longer surrender this country or its people to the false song of globalism,"[8] Trump has said, while also calling the North American Treaty

Organization (NATO), the cornerstone of U.S. and European security policy, "obsolete."[9]

At his immediate disposal, President Donald Trump has unfettered control of the drone program, the NSA's global surveillance network, Guantanamo Bay prison and its tribunal system, and even the remnants of Bush's torture program. Based on his own statements and his potential Cabinet picks for national security posts, he seemingly intends to exploit all of these tools, and more. "Foreign combatants will be tried in military commissions"[10] and Guantanamo Bay will stay open so he can "load it up with some bad dudes."[11]

Trump said he is in favor of using torture because "torture works," despite overwhelming evidence to the contrary. Due to the limitations on torture imposed by Congress and the Obama Administration, Trump has pledged to "strengthen" the law to permit waterboarding. "I would bring back a hell of a lot worse than waterboarding,"[12] Trump has also promised. Trump's pick for national security advisor, Michael Flynn, believes that U.S. interrogators should have "as many options on the table right up until the last possible minute."[13] Trump's choice for attorney general, Senator Jeff Sessions, voted against legislation seeking to limit CIA interrogation methods outlined in the Army Field Manual and railed against the closure of Guantanamo Bay.

Trump has been clearer about his plans for domestic surveillance. During his campaign he called himself the "law and order candidate"[14] and supported giving law enforcement the tools it required to access digital communications. Trump has pledged to spy on religious groups and other popular movements within the United States. He has called the Black Lives Matter organization a "threat" that, "at a minimum, we're going to have to be watching."[15] American Muslims, he said, should also take note: "I want surveillance of certain mosques."[16] Trump's pick for CIA director, Mike Pompeo, has supported wide-scale NSA surveillance and a repeal of the NSA reforms instituted under Obama. Michael Flynn has called Islam a "vicious cancer inside the body of 1.7 billion people"[17] and expressed support for forcing American Muslims to register with the government.

Trump has called Obama's Iran deal "a disaster" and vowed to "dismantle" it on day one of his administration.[18] For his part, Mike Pompeo wrote on Twitter, "I look forward to rolling back this disastrous deal with the world's largest state sponsor of terrorism."[19] Reneging on the deal would mean re-imposing economic sanctions on Iran, which could adversely affect the global oil market, raise prices, and potentially reignite Iran's nuclear weapons program. Meanwhile, both Pompeo and Flynn have expressed a support for "regime change" in Iran.

WHAT YOU CAN DO

DONATE TO PROGRESSIVE THINK TANKS OR SUBSCRIBE TO THEIR NEWSLETTERS.
Think tanks are research centers that seek to influence and shape American foreign policy. Many politicians rely on these organizations to piece together an informed view of the world. Some important think tanks that deal in foreign policy include:

Human Rights Watch (www.hrw.org)

Center for American Progress
(www.americanprogress.org)

Economic Policy Institute
(www.epi.org)

Woodrow Wilson International Center for Scholars
(www.wilsoncenter.org)

Inter-American Dialogue (www.thedialogue.org)

VOLUNTEER. The organization Citizens for Global Solutions works to support its vision of a peaceful, free, just, and sustainable world community. It is looking for campus representatives, bloggers, and social media enthusiasts to help spread the word (www.globalsolutions.org).

The World Affairs Council of America seeks to educate people about what's going on in the rest of the world "so that our communities can better compete, collaborate, and make informed decisions in a complex world." You can join your local council chapter—or start your own if one doesn't already exist (www.worldaffairscouncils.org).

Amnesty International is one of the world's leading human rights organizations and is always looking for volunteers to take part in direct actions such as protests, or to support the cause with more skilled services including letter writing, translation, press monitoring, and fund-raising (www.amnesty.org).

Americans for Informed Democracy is a student organization that brings together people on college campuses around the country to foster dialogue, hold issue-based conferences, host speakers and film screenings, and to raise awareness about issues affecting global youth. If you're a student, you can join your local chapter or start your own (www.ampglobal youth.org).

TRAVEL: One of the best ways to understand international relationships is to go make some of your own. If you can afford it, try to visit another country. Staying informed is important, but making a friend from another culture is more fun and broadens your perspective.

BOOKS TO READ:

Drift: The Unmooring of American Military Power by Rachel
   Maddow (Broadway Books, 2013). How our country

has seemingly become at peace with being in a state of perpetual war.

National Insecurity: American Leadership in an Age of Fear by David Rothkopf (PublicAffairs, 2016). An in-depth account of how 9/11 affected American foreign policy, drawn from more than 100 exclusive interviews with top national security officials.

No Place to Hide: Edward Snowden, the NSA, and the U.S. Surveillance State by Glenn Greenwald (Picador, 2015). An examination of the NSA's overreaching actions and the threat of the U.S. surveillance state.

Rise to Globalism: American Foreign Policy Since 1938 by Stephen E. Ambrose and Douglas G. Brinkley (Penguin, 2010). An overview of American foreign policy from 1938 through the Bush Administration and how key decisions and events have led its evolution.

The Way of the Knife: The CIA, a Secret Army, and a War at the Ends of the Earth by Mark Manzetti (Penguin, 2014). An examination of the history and impact of U.S. covert operations revealing the inner operations of the CIA.

"If you can't take care of your sick in the country, forget it, it's all over. I mean, it's no good. So I'm very liberal when it comes to health care. I believe in universal health care. I believe in whatever it takes to make people well and better."

—Donald Trump.[1]

"ObamaCare is a total disaster. Hillary Clinton wants to save it by making it even more expensive. Doesn't work, I will REPEAL AND REPLACE!"

—@realDonaldTrump[2]

OBAMACARE

THE BACKGROUND

Newscaster Walter Cronkite once said, "America's health care system is neither healthy, caring, nor a system." American medicine is advanced and occasionally miraculous—but it is not cheap.

There have been numerous attempts to make health care more affordable. President Harry Truman pushed the first serious proposal in 1945, telling Congress just seven months into his presidency, "Millions of our citizens do not now have a full measure of opportunity to achieve and enjoy good health. . . . The time has arrived for action to help them attain that opportunity and that protection." The concept of universal health coverage was popular with the American public, but actually paying for it was another story. After the federal government effectively took over private industry to support the war effort, Congress did not want to open its purse strings for yet another government program. The American Medical Association, which opposed universal coverage, exploited the fear of advancing Communism and condemned Truman's bill as "socialized medicine." Meanwhile, Southern Democrats balked at the prospect of federally funded hospitals treating blacks alongside whites. After Republicans seized control of Congress during the 1946 midterm elections, Truman's dream of universal health care evaporated.

Two decades later, however, President Lyndon B. Johnson muscled two new government health programs through Congress: Medicare and Medicaid (see the chapter on Entitlement Programs, page 63). While the programs did not offer universal health coverage for all Americans, Medicare covered seniors over sixty-five and Medicaid offered basic care for the impoverished. (Fittingly, Harry Truman became Medicare's first beneficiary after receiving the first Medicare card.) Nevertheless, the majority of Americans remained at the mercy of the rates health insurance companies chose to charge.

The next best chance for reform came during the 1970s under the administration of President Richard M. Nixon, a Republican. As a teenager, Nixon had watched two of his brothers die—one from encephalitis, the other from tuberculosis. Against the wishes of his party, Nixon proposed subsidies to assist low-income Americans in buying insurance, along with a mandate that employers purchase insurance for their employees. "Without adequate health care, no one can make full use of his or her talents and opportunities," Nixon said. Though his plan was not true universal coverage, it would have made affordable health insurance a possibility for the more than half of Americans under sixty-five who lacked it.

Ironically, Nixon's plan was scuttled by a liberal Democratic senator named Edward M. Kennedy, who did not believe Nixon's plan went far enough. Instead, Kennedy wanted a genuine single-payer health care program that did not rely on private insurance companies. Just as Kennedy and Nixon were nearing a compromise, the Watergate scandal hit. Kennedy walked away from the deal, hoping he could engineer a better plan in the wake of Nixon's self-destruction. He did not. "That was the best deal we were going to get," Kennedy later lamented.

Bill Clinton made health care key to his 1992 presidential campaign, promising affordable universal coverage. After the election he tasked his wife, Hillary Rodham Clinton, with drafting the reform plan. The final draft was unwieldy: At more than one thousand pages, the bill she helped craft was centered around an employer mandate to provide health insurance for employees, a ban on refusing coverage due to preexisting conditions, and subsidies for those too poor to afford coverage. The legislation faced enormous opposition, especially from insurance companies. After Republicans won the House and Senate with the 1994 midterm elections, the Clintons admitted defeat.

WHAT DID OBAMA DO?

Sweeping into office in 2008 promising hope and change, President Obama directed his staff to begin drafting the Affordable Care Act, instantly and forever known as Obamacare to foes and allies alike. The law set minimum coverage standards for care, required large employers to provide insurance for employees, allowed young adults to remain on their parents' plan until age twenty-six, vastly expanded Medicaid to cover low-income people, and most important, instituted a ban on preexisting condition rules. For the first time, insurers were forced to accept all applicants, no matter how sick they were.

To offset the costs of sick patients, Obamacare included a mandate that all individuals not covered by employer plans, Medicare, or Medicaid purchase private health insurance through government-run marketplaces, called exchanges. The law also provided subsidies to make insurance affordable, averaging $291 per month. Though extremely controversial, the individual mandate was the linchpin of Obamacare. Without young, healthy people purchasing insurance to offset the heavy costs incurred by the sick, premiums would skyrocket.

Obama succeeded in passing the Affordable Care Act despite zero Republican support, though Senate Democrats ultimately had to use an arcane procedure known as budget reconciliation to bypass a Republican filibuster with a simple majority vote. (This parliamentary maneuver may come back to haunt Democrats, as Republicans can now use the same tactic to repeal much of Obamacare.) The Senate passed the finalized Affordable Care act on December 24, 2009; the House, on March 21, 2010.

Since the law was first implemented in 2014, the uninsured rate has dropped by nearly half. By 2016, the National Health Interview Survey revealed, the rate had fallen to 8.6 percent, a record low. The change was even starker in poorer states, such as Arkansas, where the uninsured rate dropped from 22.5 percent to 9.6 percent. Since the law's passage, the uninsured rate has been cut in half nationwide. Obamacare survived two major court challenges, but the Supreme Court dealt it one blow: States could choose not to expand Medicaid.

Obamacare is not without its problems. For example, premiums in many states are rising sharply. The Obama Administration admitted that premiums on health care exchanges would increase by an average of 25 percent in 2017. However, this statistic is misleading. Americans on Medicare and Medicaid will not see this premium increase, nor will people who receive insurance through their employers. Americans who receive subsidies through exchanges will also not be affected. Only those who purchase insurance through exchanges but make too much money to qualify for a subsidy will be affected—fewer than two million people, or one half of 1 percent of the American population. There are many ways to fix this problem, such as allowing people over fifty-five to buy into Medicare early, or creating a public, government-run plan.

WHAT MIGHT DONALD TRUMP DO?

Where does Trump stand on health care? The better question is, where does Trump stand on health care *at any moment?* The forty-fifth president has taken multiple positions. He seems to hate Obamacare, but he occasionally approves of the mandate requiring that all Americans buy health insurance: "I like the mandate . . . I don't want people dying on the streets,"[3] he said in February 2016. Sometimes, though, he doesn't like it: "Our elected representatives must eliminate the individual mandate. No person should be required to buy insurance unless he or she wants to,"[4] his official campaign website states. Before the election, he was all in on repealing Obamacare: "On day one of the Trump Administration, we will ask Congress to immediately deliver a full repeal of Obamacare."[5] But after the election? "Either Obamacare will be amended, or repealed and replaced,"[6] the president-elect mused to the *Wall Street Journal* in November 2016.

So what will Trump do when he takes office? No one knows for sure, but given that the Republican Congress tried and failed to repeal Obamacare more than sixty times—once, fittingly, on Groundhog Day—it's not hard to guess what will happen. Trump's pick to lead the Department of Health and Human Services, Georgia representative Tom Price, is an ardent foe of Obamacare. As Price said in 2011: "The purpose of health reform should be to advance accessibility, affordability, quality, responsiveness, and innovation. None of these are improved" by the Affordable Care Act.[7]

In the worst-case scenario, Trump and Congress can *mostly* repeal Obamacare. While sixty Senate votes are normally required to break a filibuster and pass (or in this case, repeal) legislation, Trump and Congress can dismantle key parts of Obamacare with a simple fifty-one vote majority, thanks to the same arcane budget reconciliation process that allowed Democrats to pass Obamacare in 2009. If Trump chooses this route, here is what will happen:

- Subsidies that make exchange health care plans affordable will end. People can still buy insurance from state and federal exchanges, but they will have to pay for it completely out of pocket.
- The employer mandate requiring large and midsize companies to provide health insurance for workers will end.

- The individual mandate requiring everyone to have insurance, and the tax levied on those who do not buy it, will end.
- The Medicaid expansion will end.

According to the Congressional Budget Office, twenty-two million people will lose health insurance. There will be a transition period—probably two years, based on previous Republican plans—so no one will lose Obamacare overnight. But without subsidies and Medicaid expansion, health insurance will simply be unaffordable for tens of millions of people.

That number could grow much bigger. Without sixty votes to overcome a Democratic filibuster, Senate Republicans cannot repeal the most critical component of Obamacare: the ban on refusing to cover preexisting conditions. Even if Republicans move forward with a partial repeal, insurance companies still must accept all applicants, from healthy twenty-year-olds who avoid doctors to cancer-stricken diabetic patients who require around-the-clock care. Obama designed the individual mandate to ensure that young, healthy people offset the costs of older, sicker people. But if only sick people are buying insurance, the entire system crumbles. After all, why pay for something before you need it? Well, imagine if there were no requirement for car insurance—people would only purchase plans from the sidewalk after causing a twelve-car pileup.

Let's say Congress only repeals the individual mandate and leaves the subsidies. This result too is possible with only a majority vote. The average premium for single people would immediately jump by 27 percent, according to the Center for American Progress. However, repealing the individual mandate *and* the subsidies "would have an even more dramatic impact and would double the single premium in the exchange to almost $16,000 per year."[8] Even a partial repeal will be devastating to countless people.

What will Trump replace Obamacare with? Depending on the day, he has "great plans" that mean "better health care, much better, for less money."[9] Trump cannot pass his own health care plan easily, but if he can, in his own words, "replace Obamacare" and "get something great,"[10] Trump has been vague about what that would actually be. His campaign website suggests age-old Republican ideas of creating high-risk pools and allowing people to buy insurance across state lines. The result? Trump might Make America Uninsured Again: According to the Committee for a Responsible Federal Budget, Trump's plan to repeal and replace Obamacare would cost $550 billion over a decade while only covering 5 percent of the twenty-two million people who would lose coverage after repealing Obamacare—effectively doubling the uninsured rate.

WHAT YOU CAN DO

SIGN UP FOR OBAMACARE. If you want Obamacare to last, and you don't have health insurance, sign up now, as hundreds of thousands of Americans have since the election. The more people who can potentially lose coverage, the more politically challenging it is for Trump and the Republican congress to repeal it. Open enrollment lasts until January 31, 2017.

DONATE TO OR VOLUNTEER FOR ENROLL AMERICA. Enroll America is the nation's leading health care enrollment coalition, working with more than 6,700 partners in all fifty states to create cutting-edge tools, analyze data, inform policy, and share best practices in service of its mission: maximizing the number of Americans who enroll in and retain health coverage under the Affordable Care Act. Since the election, it has doubled down on its efforts to make it as politically difficult as possible for Trump to repeal Obamacare (www.enrollamerica.org).

DONATE TO OR VOLUNTEER FOR FAMILIES USA. Families USA, one of the key advocacy groups that helped pass the Affordable Care Act in 2009, is dedicated to the achievement of high-quality, affordable health care and improved health for all. Families USA advances its mission through public-policy analysis, advocacy, and collaboration with partners to promote a patient- and community-centered health system. Ron Pollack, the executive director of Families USA, is forming the Coalition to Keep America Covered, which focuses on educating people about the effects of repealing Obamacare. The Coalition is prepared to wage a multiyear campaign to keep Americans covered by any means necessary. In the meantime, sign the petition to protect America's health coverage (http://familiesusa.org/protect-americas-health-coverage).

EDUCATE FRIENDS AND FAMILY ABOUT OBAMACARE. Though many Americans don't support Obamacare, they largely support its provisions. According to a Reuters/Ipsos poll, 61 percent of respondents favor allowing young adults to stay on their parents' insurance plan until age twenty-six. Seventy-two percent of respondents approve of the provision requiring medium and large companies to provide insurance for their employees. Eighty-two percent of respondents favored banning insurance companies from denying coverage to people with preexisting conditions.

It can be difficult explaining why Obamacare is so vital without sounding wonkish, but you can keep it simple: Without it, twenty-two million people will lose their health care. Without it, the sick will be unable to find the care they require. Without it, the most vulnerable people will not be able to afford what many consider a basic human right. If your friends and family agree this shouldn't happen, urge them to join you in calling your representatives and donating to the above organizations.

If Obamacare is repealed, do not panic. Nothing is likely to happen overnight. If you receive subsidies through exchanges or are enrolled in the Medicaid expansion, you will not lose your coverage immediately. If you qualify for traditional Medicaid, you should not be affected by an Obamacare repeal. (However, Trump and Republicans *do* want to drastically overhaul Medicaid and Medicare. See the chapter on Entitlement Programs on page 63 for more information.) During the transition period, you have time to work with the above organizations to figure out your next steps. More important, you have time to fight back.

BOOKS TO READ

America's Bitter Pill: Money, Politics, Backroom Deals, and the Fight to Fix Our Broken Healthcare System by Steven Brill (Random House, 2015). The writing of, the implementation of, and the changes that Obamacare is bringing to the health care industry.

The Healing of America: A Global Quest for Better, Cheaper, and Fairer Health Care by T. R. Reid (Penguin, 2010). Contrasting Obamacare with the universal health care systems in France, Germany, Japan, the UK, and Canada.

Reinventing American Health Care: How the Affordable Care Act Will Improve Our Terribly Complex, Blatantly Unjust, Outrageously Expensive, Grossly Inefficient, Error Prone System by Ezekiel J. Emanuel (PublicAffairs 2015). An insider's persuasive and explanatory pro-Obamacare guide to the complex legislation that lays out the stakes and the changes that will be needed for its success.

Remedy and Reaction: The Peculiar American Struggle over Health Care Reform by Paul Starr (Yale University Press, 2013). A history of U.S. health care—whom it helps, hurts, and enriches, and how difficult it will be to become effective in our current political climate.

"Our very weak and ineffective leader, Paul Ryan, had a bad conference call where his members went wild at his disloyalty."

—@realDonald Trump [1]

"The World Trade Center came down during the reign of George Bush. He kept us safe? That is not safe."

—Donald Trump [2]

POLITICAL ISSUES

THE BACKGROUND

Bitter political divisions have been part of American history since our nation's birth. Our Founding Fathers claimed to oppose partisanship and political parties, but even before the end of George Washington's presidency these same Founding Fathers adopted them.

Some of the earliest and most acrimonious divisions occurred when Alexander Hamilton's Federalist Party advocated a strong federal government, while Thomas Jefferson's and James Madison's Democratic-Republicans opposed such centralization. Soon the partisanship between these parties escalated to Federalists attacking Jefferson as godless. One newspaper declared that Jefferson would create a nation where "murder, robbery, rape, adultery and incest will openly be taught and practiced," and Republicans supposedly called John Adams a hermaphrodite. Adams' staff responded by calling Jefferson "a mean-spirited, low-lived fellow, the son of a half-breed Indian squaw, sired by a Virginia mulatto father."

These early partisans also understood the power of manipulating district boundaries. In 1788, Patrick Henry and other anti-Federalists redrew Virginia's congressional map in an attempt to deny James Madison a seat in the U.S. Congress. In 1812, Massachusetts governor Elbridge Gerry signed a bill that took redrawing the state's district lines to such extremes that one district looked like a salamander. The term "gerrymander" was born and has been used ever since to describe this practice.

By 1829, the Republican party had split into Jacksonian Democrats—favoring the presidency and opposing the Bank of the United States—and Whigs favoring Congress and the modernization of the banking system. Twenty-five years later, the Whigs had dissolved and become Republicans. In 1860, Abraham Lincoln won the party the presidency, solidifying Republican themes of modernization and expansion.

Slavery, however, most clearly differentiated the new Republicans and the Democrats. In 1869, Republicans helped pass the Fifteenth Amendment to the U.S. Constitution, which gave the right to vote to African American men. Thereafter, blacks were a staple faction of the Republicans, and southern whites left the party in droves for the Democrats.

Republicans expanded their support during the Progressive Era of the late nineteenth and early twentieth centuries by advocating trust-busting, labor unions, and political reform, and Democrats, with a base of laissez-faire easterners and poor southern white and western farmers, struggled to win elections. (1920 marked the ratification of the Nineteenth Amendment to the U.S. Constitution, giving women the right to vote, though initially this had little impact on the two parties' balance.)

The Great Depression and the 1932 election of Franklin Roosevelt and his New Deal, with its deployment of a robust federal government, transformed the two parties. Roosevelt's Democratic Party built a dominant coalition of organized labor, minorities, white southerners, populist farm groups, and intellectuals, while Republicans, isolationist and anti–New Deal, lost seven of nine presidential elections.

Even as the New Deal Democrats became more integrated, southern whites remained aligned with the party—that is, until Lyndon Johnson's sweeping civil rights measures of the mid-1960s. "We have lost the South for a generation," Johnson reportedly told an aide after signing the 1964 Civil Rights Act. (It has turned out to last quite longer than that, as the South today is strongly Republican with no change in sight.) Richard Nixon exploited this shift in his elections of 1968 and 1972.

The 1980s saw Ronald Reagan create a new, winning coalition for the Republican Party composed of evangelicals and fiscal conservatives. While Bill Clinton later used a more centrist Democratic Party to win the White House, the 1980s and

'90s, with their supercharged Supreme Court confirmations, House Speaker Newt Gingrich's scorched-earth congressional leadership, and the impeachment of Clinton, laid the groundwork for today's hyperpartisanship.

With George W. Bush's election to the White House, Republicans used hot-button social issues like abortion and gay marriage to add working-class whites to Reagan's coalition, and hyperpartisanship continued to deepen. Bush appointed far-right conservatives to the Supreme Court who returned the favor by gutting voting rights enforcement and campaign finance reform; newly Republican strongholds like Texas used redistricting to all but lock out Democratic opposition.

While Barack Obama's charisma and message of hope created a coalition of new young voters and traditional Democrats, backlash against his race and GOP-cultivated anti-government sentiment spawned the Tea Party movement, which promotes the use of as little federal power as possible— all of which ultimately gave rise to Donald Trump, who derided Republicans almost as much as Democrats, and who defied most of the rules of modern politics.

WHAT DID BARACK OBAMA DO?

As of mid-November 2016, Barack Obama had an approval rating similar to that of Ronald Reagan when he left office. Despite this popularity, Obama's presidency did little to strengthen the Democratic Party. Part of this may be due to his measured, conciliatory style. During many of his biggest congressional fights—like the American Recovery and Reinvestment Act, the Affordable Care Act, and the 2011 "grand bargain," regarding budget and tax cuts—Obama was willing to compromise, opting to do what he thought best for the outcome of the legislation versus what would score political points.

Additionally, Obama always seemed averse to the conventional glad-handing and arm-twisting synonymous with the Washington political process. Where his more politically inclined predecessors, like Bill Clinton or George W. Bush, relished this personal lobbying, Obama avoided the schmoozing that might have helped to consolidate Democratic power.

Beyond partisan politics, in the areas of voter participation and campaign finance reform, Obama had little effect, largely because of the conservative-majority Supreme Court. The 2010 Supreme Court decision *Citizens United v. Federal Election Commission,* and the subsequent *SpeechNow.org v. FEC* and *McCutcheon v. FEC,* removed most of the restraints for controlling the flood of private and corporate money that distorts the political process. And while Obama started out saying he would work to overturn Citizens United, nothing ever came of this. Additionally, in 2008 Obama became the first presidential candidate of a major party in a general election to decline participation in the public funding of presidential campaigns, established in 1976. He did the same in 2012, both decisions made for pragmatic reasons but with symbolic consequences. Many campaign finance reformers were disheartened when, in 2012, Obama abandoned his previous refusal of corporate donations to finance his inauguration festivities, and his campaign organization was converted into an advocacy group able to raise unrestricted amounts.

Where Obama's administration worked very hard was in the field of voter participation, especially in defending the 1965 Voting Rights Act (VRA). Despite the conservative-majority Supreme Court gutting important parts of the VRA in 2013's *Shelby County v. Holder*, Obama's Justice Department filed more than forty cases and participated in another sixty to defend the VRA, including successful cases in Texas, North Carolina, and Florida.

WHAT MIGHT DONALD TRUMP DO?

Donald Trump's campaign was as much an indictment of traditional Republican politics as those of Democrats, and the coalition that put him in office didn't fit the usual political boundaries. Nonetheless, his election has allied him with traditional Republican political machines, especially in Congress. Though this may give him considerable power, it could also isolate him from his base, which distrusts the establishment of any party.

Trump has given all indications that he intends to appoint conservative judges who will further erode voter participation and campaign finance reform. He has given lip service to condemning the role of so-called super PACs, which can raise unlimited sums of money to advocate for candidates, but his Republican allies in Congress show no interest in imposing the restrictions necessary to control them. Trump's choice for attorney general, Jeff Sessions of Alabama, who was previously denied a federal judgeship because of allegations of racist comments and who has called the VRA "a piece of intrusive legislation,"[3] is highly unlikely to pursue enforcement of the VRA as Eric Holder and Loretta Lynch, Obama's attorneys general, did.

Furthermore, on the campaign trail Trump endlessly flogged the myth of voter fraud: "Voter fraud is very, very common,"[4] and "people that have died ten years ago are still voting."[5] Most election experts say the kind of voter fraud Trump is talking about—voter impersonation—is exceedingly rare; certainly not common enough to affect a presidential election. Instead, the term has been used for years by Republicans to agitate for stricter ID laws, which have been shown to decrease participation at the polls by marginalized voters.

WHAT YOU CAN DO

FIGHT HARD IN THE 2018 MIDTERM ELECTIONS. Perhaps the best way to fight the Trump Administration is for the Democrats to take back as many seats as possible in 2018 state and congressional races. The first midterm election after a presidential election often goes for the opposition party. Obama's Democrats lost sixty-three House and six Senate seats in 2010; 2006 lost Bush's GOP thirty House and six Senate seats; and the GOP lost twenty-six House seats in 1982 and eight Senate seats in 1986, during Reagan's presidency. Republicans will hold a forty-five-seat majority in the House next session and a four-seat majority in the Senate, including a Louisiana runoff in December that Republicans are expected to win. Although far more Democrats than Republicans are up for reelection in the Senate, and gerrymandered House seats make a takeover of the House difficult, it is still possible to reclaim both chambers—but only if people work for it. On the state level, thirty-six governors and forty-six legislatures will have races. These will be crucial not only for maintaining state government independence from the Trump agenda but for preparing for the 2020 redistricting cycle that maps congressional areas for the next decade. If Trump is unable to deliver on his many promises, by the second year of his administration there's a good chance he will have lost the goodwill that swept him into office.

GET INVOLVED LOCALLY. Create alliances with your friends, neighbors, and community members to watch what's happening politically in your community. If you don't like what you're seeing, the path to vote Trump out of office in four years starts in communities like yours. Neighbors need to be convinced, fresh candidates need to be chosen, new voters need to be identified and engaged, and American values of pluralism, inclusion, and fairness need to be protected. Remember that America's government was never intended to be a totally federal government, but one with powerful state and local governments as well. Social conservatives, in their well-organized fights against reproductive rights and marriage equality, have shown us how we can use this structure to resist federal actions.

HELP THE DEMOCRATIC PARTY CHANGE. Though many people have become exasperated with the Democratic Party, it remains the only real opposition to Trump. Still, the party will have to change as a result of the 2016 elections, and the best way to influence that change is to let it how you feel. You can do this on the local level, or you can use tools like social media as well as old-fashioned mail and phone calls to communicate with all levels of the party's leadership. You can start with these websites:

www.democrats.org—the Democratic National Committee's website

www.asdc.democrats.org/state-parties—links   to   state
Democratic parties

IDENTIFY AND SUPPORT STRONG CANDIDATES IN THE DISTRICTS THAT MATTER. If
you're in one of these districts, you will have the opportunity
to volunteer for races that could switch the balance of power.
Volunteer! But even if you aren't, you can get involved with the
campaigns that are potential game changers by signing petitions, contributing money, and, as many have done in these
last few elections, traveling to these districts to work with local leaders.

COMPLAIN. Despite talk of echo chambers and social media bub-
bles, use any appropriate opportunities to share with your
family, friends, and (online and offline) communities Trump's
failures to deliver on promises or to maintain the standards of
American governance. The more you talk, the more likely you
are to be heard.

SUPPORT ORGANIZATIONS THAT WORK FOR FAIR GOVERNANCE. The League of
Women Voters is the venerable voting organization founded in
1920 when women achieved the right to vote. Besides its long-
standing work for campaign finance reform and against voter
ID laws, the League's structure relies on a robust network of
local chapters that make it easy for both women and men to
get involved (www.lwv.org).

Common Cause is a nonprofit, nonpartisan organization promoting open, honest, and accountable government with offices in thirty-five states. It has a long history of supporting campaign finance reform and voting rights, and is currently working to amend the Constitution to reverse Citizens United. It has also filed suit in North Carolina to block political gerrymandering in what is hoped will be a precedent-setting case (www.commoncause.org).

The Brennan Center for Justice is a nonpartisan law and policy institute based out of New York University School of Law that seeks to improve our systems of democracy and justice, including voting rights and campaign finance reform. It has worked hard to fight voter restrictions, and it is working with Common Cause on its suit against North Carolina's gerrymandering (www.brennancenter.org).

The American Civil Liberties Union Voting Rights Project applies the ACLU's brand of advocacy to the protection of the 1965 Voting Rights Act and the gains it has brought to minority communities. The Project's current focuses include fighting gerrymandering and voter ID laws, criminal re-enfranchisement, and making it easier for more people to vote (www.aclu.org/issues/voting-rights).

Project Vote is a national nonpartisan, nonprofit organization that works to mobilize marginalized and underrepresented voters. It first came to many people's attention in 1992 when Barack Obama ran a successful voter registration drive in Chicago. Since then it has continued to advocate for greater participation by low-income and minority voters (www.proj ectvote.org).

The National Democratic Redistricting Committee is a new project that will be chaired by former attorney general Eric Holder and Obama has identified it as a group he will work with when he leaves office. It will coordinate campaign strategies, help fund-raise, organize ballot initiatives, and challenge state redistricting maps.

BOOKS TO READ:

Dark Money: The Hidden History of the Billionaires Behind the Rise of the Radical Right by Jane Mayer (Doubleday, 2016).
A meticulously researched narrative tracing the money spent by these citizens and its impact on American politics.

Ratf**ked: The True Story Behind the Secret Plan to Steal America's Democracy by David Daley (Liveright, 2016).
How Republican operatives have worked to reshape state politics and alter the electoral map with dark money.

Strangers in Their Own Land: Anger and Mourning on the American Right by Arlie Russell Hochschild (The New Press, 2016).
An explanation of impoverished red-state Americans

and why they fight seemingly beneficial government
intervention.

The Unwinding: An Inner History of the New America by George
Packer (Farrar, Straus and Giroux, 2014). An ambitious,
novelistic account of several Americans finding new paths
in a rapidly changing country.

"It's certainly not groundbreaking news that the early victories by the women on *The Apprentice* were, to a very large extent, dependent on their sex appeal."

—Donald Trump [1]

WOMEN'S ISSUES

THE BACKGROUND

America's Founding Fathers declared that "All men are created equal"—"men" being the operative word. The birthright of a white eighteenth-century male was head of household, industry, and government. Women were wives and mothers, valued for their caretaking skills and appearance. A girl's father, and later her husband, maintained enormous control over her life.

Because women were considered emotionally and physically fragile, state and federal laws were created to "protect" them from the world outside their home. For nearly a century after the Declaration of Independence, an American woman could not, among other things, own or inherit property in her own name (Mississippi was the first state to allow it, in 1839) or open a bank account (California, 1862).

Women also faced serious health risks. Few contraceptive options existed, and due to a lack of modern medical training and sanitary practices, maternal and infant mortality were common. Although abortion in the U.S. was legal in early pregnancy when the Constitution was adopted, by the mid-nineteenth century states began restricting it. By 1910, all but one state had criminalized abortion except when necessary to save the mother's life.

Pivotal changes in women's legal and cultural standing finally arrived thanks to the efforts of three distinct waves of feminism: movements based on the theory of the political, economic, and social equality of the sexes. The first milestone was achieving the right to vote, known as suffrage. The initial push for suffrage began at a meeting of abolitionists led by Elizabeth Cady Stanton and Lucretia Mott in Seneca Falls, New York, in 1848. Determining that the best way to ensure the right was passage of a constitutional amendment, in 1869, Stanton, along with Susan B. Anthony, founded the National Woman Suffrage Association. (In an odd historical coincidence, Stanton's husband, Henry Brewster Stanton, was a co-founder of the Republican Party.)

In 1916, after nearly fifty years of being rebuffed, activists in the National Woman's Party led by Alice Paul took more radical measures, holding hunger strikes and picketing the White House daily. By 1919, the Nineteenth Amendment passed both houses of Congress and was sent to the states for ratification. In August 1920, Tennessee state representative Harry Burn, at the prompting of his mother, cast the deciding vote.

The second feminist wave coincided with the civil rights movement. Women, who had done their part working in factories during World War II while male soldiers fought abroad, wanted more than to resume their role as happy homemakers. Accomplishments of this era include the first federal Equal Pay Act, which took effect in 1963; the elimination of sex-segregated employment ads, in 1968; the ability of a married woman to hold a credit card in her own name, in 1974; and the right (and responsibility) to serve on a jury, by 1975. In 1960, the Food and Drug Administration approved the hormonal birth-control pill, which has since been credited with a dramatic drop in unplanned pregnancies. The right for married couples to use it, however, wasn't solidified until the 1965 Supreme Court *Griswold v. Connecticut* decision. The court extended that right to single women in 1972. After 1978, a woman could no longer be fired for becoming pregnant and, in 1980, the Equal Employment Opportunity Commission finally established federal legal recourse for sexual harassment.

This disjointed progress ran parallel with the ongoing efforts, since 1923, to establish a federal Equal Rights Amendment. It states simply, "Equality of rights under the law shall not be denied or abridged by the United States or by any state on account of sex." Led by the National Organization for Women and the eighty-organization coalition ERAmerica, the would-be Twenty-Seventh Amendment finally passed both houses of Congress in 1972 and was sent to the states for ratification with the usual seven-year deadline, later extended until 1982. But by then, Ronald Reagan had been elected on a conservative Republican platform and the amendment stalled—however, organizations such as ERA Action (www.eraaction.org) are still working hard to pass it in the final few states needed, as are individuals such as Congresswoman Carolyn B. Maloney (D-NY).

Meanwhile, women could not legally obtain an abortion in two-thirds of the states for much of the twentieth century. The right to choose only became available to all American women following the 1973 *Roe v. Wade* Supreme Court case, brought by a woman who tried to obtain an abortion in Texas, where it was illegal except to save the mother's life. As the National Abortion Federation put it, the court deemed that "Americans' right to privacy included the right of a woman to decide whether to have children, and the right of a woman and her doctor to make that decision without state interference."

The third wave of feminism came in the late twentieth century and coincided with the idea that women should be able to, as the media described it, "have it all"—i.e., both a career and a family. This movement emerged in response to the rise of the anti-feminist stances of the religious right as well as welfare reform under President Bill Clinton, which made it more difficult for single mothers to access federal entitlements, and coincided with efforts to make feminism more racially and economically diverse.

Today, even as more women than men graduate from college and take on roles from astronaut to secretary of state, women still lag behind men in many areas. For instance, on average, women earn only 79 cents for every dollar a man earns. Or, as *Forbes* reported, only 4 percent of Fortune 500 CEOs are female. And, as recent events have proved, there has yet to be a female president of the United States.

WHAT DID BARACK OBAMA DO?

The very first piece of legislation President Obama signed was the Lilly Ledbetter Fair Pay Act, which stated that each discriminatory paycheck resets the period of time during which a worker may file a claim of pay discrimination on the basis of sex, race, national origin, age, religion, and disability. Within months of taking office, Obama established the White House Council on Women and Girls, composed of representatives from each federal agency and White House office and tasked with ensuring that "the needs of women and girls are taken into account in all programs, policies, and legislation."[2]

Obama's tenure included widespread appointments of diverse women throughout government, including more female members of his cabinet (eight) than any previous president.

Both of Obama's nominees to the Supreme Court—Sonia Sotomayor and Elena Kagan—were women.

Obama's signature domestic accomplishment, the Affordable Care Act, has benefited women in many ways. First, it put an end to the practice of gender rating, under which insurers routinely charged women up to 50 percent more than men for monthly premiums. The ACA also included a suite of guaranteed essential health benefits for women, including maternity coverage (previously available in only a small number of private health plans) and preventive services such as mammograms. And it covered screenings for diseases and conditions that disproportionately affect women, including alcohol addiction, depression, certain cancers, and sexually transmitted infections. Most notably, the ACA requires full coverage for all FDA-approved forms of birth control. Planned Parenthood estimates that thirty million women have benefited from these provisions.

Here is a brief list of other initiatives benefitting women under the Obama Administration:

- Opening ground combat positions in the U.S. military to women and initiating programs to assist female veterans and ensure justice for victims of sexual assault.
- Strengthening various efforts on behalf of low-

income mothers and their children, including
increased funding for Head Start, a government
program that provides comprehensive early
childhood education, health, nutrition, and
parenting services.

- Overseeing initiatives to support women-owned
businesses, including training and counseling
services and access to federal contracts credit.
This led to what the White House called "historic
levels" of lending to women-owned businesses.

- Strengthened Title IX of the Education
Amendments of 1972, which protects people
from gender discrimination in education
programs and activities that receive federal
financial assistance.

WHAT MIGHT DONALD TRUMP DO?

Trump has claimed that "Nobody respects women more than
I do. Nobody."[3] But he has said relatively little about his actual
plans on women's issues.

However, he has tipped his hand on his general attitudes
toward women through his public statements. He once said
"Putting a wife to work is a very dangerous thing. . . . When I
come home and dinner's not ready, I go through the roof."[4] As

for sexual assault of women in the military, he once tweeted, "What did these geniuses expect when they put men & women together?"[5]

Trump's campaign nearly sank when leaked 2006 footage from TV's *Access Hollywood* caught him bragging to host Billy Bush that his fame and fortune allowed him to sexually assault women: "I just start kissing them without even asking," he said. "I grab them by the pussy—and they let you do it."[6] Afterward, more than a dozen women, including a *People* magazine reporter, came forward alleging past incidents like those Trump described.

Trump has also referred to a breast-feeding executive as "disgusting,"[7] disparaged a Latina former Miss Universe who'd gained a bit of weight as "Miss Piggy" and "Miss Housekeeping,"[8] and labeled his presidential opponent "a nasty woman."[9] He's called ordinary and famous females alike pigs, dogs, and slobs. When Fox News' Megyn Kelly challenged this behavior, he later told CNN's Don Lemon, "You could see there was blood coming out of her eyes, blood coming out of her . . . wherever."[10]

In his first hundred days, Trump has pledged to replace the late Supreme Court Justice Antonin Scalia with a pro-life judge who will overturn *Roe v. Wade*, leaving abortion rights up to the states, as it was before 1973. Trump said on the campaign trail that women who have abortions where it's illegal should face "some form of punishment."[11] Otherwise, as he told *60 Minutes'* Lesley Stahl, they can always "go to another state."[12]

WHAT YOU CAN DO

DONATE, particularly to women's reproductive health organizations. Give to Planned Parenthood (www.plannedparenthood.org), which provides services in every state, and the Guttmacher Institute (www.guttmacher.org), which focuses on research, and/or NARAL Pro-Choice America (www.naral.org), which performs advocacy. You can also volunteer to accompany women visiting Planned Parenthood or other women's health clinics, who may face picketers and verbal harassment.

JOIN ONE OF THE LARGE NATIONAL WOMEN'S RIGHTS ORGANIZATIONS, such as the National Organization for Women (www.now.org), which has several chapters in all fifty states. Sign up for news updates and/or apply for a project grant from the Ms. Foundation for Women (www.forwomen.org). Its goal, "to build women's collective power to realize a nation of justice for all," emphasizes concerns of women of color and low-income women. There are also major women's and gender-equity groups—some international—whose work you can get involved with, follow, or support, from the American Association of University Women (www.aauw.org) to the YWCA (www.ywca.org).

JOIN AND SUPPORT THE LEAGUE OF WOMEN VOTERS. Established shortly before the Nineteenth Amendment was ratified, the nonpartisan League initially helped twenty million women carry out their new responsibilities as voters. Today it continues to pursue its mission of encouraging informed and active participation in government, increasing understanding of major public policy issues, and influencing public policy through education and advocacy. There are numerous chapters in every state (www.lwv.org).

DONATE TO GROUPS THAT WORK TO GET WOMEN ELECTED TO OFFICE, such as EMILY's List (www.emilyslist.org), which supports pro-choice Democrats for Congress and helped elect the latest female additions to the U.S. Senate, including Tammy Duckworth of Illinois. Or you can work on the campaigns of your preferred pro-equality candidates.

MONITOR THE NEWS AND ENTERTAINMENT MEDIA FOR SEXISM and/or create your own media. For example, you can join Women Action and the Media (www.womenactionmedia.org) or donate to and follow Women in Media and News (www.wimnonline.org).

USE SOCIAL MEDIA TO PROMOTE WOMEN'S RIGHTS AND WOMEN'S HEALTH in every way you can. Call out online misogyny and harassment.

Hollaback! (www.ihollaback.org) encourages people to take photos and videos of the perpetrators of street harassment with a special app and post them online.

READ PUBLICATIONS to learn more about women's issues and what you can do. Besides the iconic *Ms.* magazine, published since 1972, check out Rewire (www.rewire.news) on reproductive health issues, or the many outlets focused on millennial readers and intersectionality, such as the online Everyday Feminism (www.everydayfeminism.com).

BOOKS TO READ

Essential Feminist Reader, edited by Estelle Freedman (Modern Library Classics, 2007). The first anthology to present the full scope of feminist history, including essays by Susan B. Anthony, Sojourner Truth, Margaret Sanger, Betty Friedan, Audre Lorde, the Guerrilla Girls, and many more.

Feminism Is for Everybody: Passionate Politics by bell hooks (2nd edition; Routledge 2014). A short, accessible primer that explores the nature of feminism and its positive promise to eliminate sexism, sexist exploitation, and oppression.

The New Feminist Agenda: Defining the Next Revolution for Women, Work, and Family by Madeleine Kunin (Chelsea Green

Publishing, 2012). A guide to understanding where women
have made gains, and where more gains are still sorely
needed, by the former governor of Vermont.

Pro: Reclaiming Abortion Rights by Katha Pollitt (Picador, 2015).
A defense of abortion rights, reframing abortion as a
common part of a woman's reproductive life.

A Vindication of the Rights of Woman by Mary Wollstonecraft
(Dover Thrift Editions, 1996; originally published 1792).
A fascinating and powerful treatise (from the mother of
the author of *Frankenstein,* Mary Shelley) on the value of
women in society.

CONCLUSION

In this book you've read about a dozen issues that are animating our country's political conversation. These topics are not necessarily the ones most important to every American, and admittedly many other vital issues affect our lives on a daily basis.

Veterans' issues, for example, may be your favorite cause. In that case, you can learn more about them from the U.S. Department of Veterans Affairs (www.va.gov); help out injured or ill military veterans and their families via the Fisher House Foundation (www.fisherhouse.org); the (sometimes criticized) Wounded Warrior Project (www.woundedwarriorproject.org); and/or volunteer at a veterans' hospital (www.dav.org).

Perhaps freedom of the press concerns you the most. There are many organizations fighting to keep our nation's media free and our journalists safe. Get in touch with the Committee to Protect Journalists (www.cpj.org) or Freedom of the Press Foundation, a nonprofit organization that promotes public-interest journalism (www.freedom.press). Or check out the Student Press Law Center, which works to help protect freedom of the press for student newspapers (www.splc.org).

If you are concerned with religious freedom (i.e., the right to practice the religion of your choice, not the right to discriminate against others in the name of it), look up the Religious Freedom Center, which educates the public on religious protections (www.religiousfreedomcenter.org), or join the American Civil Liberties Union (www.aclu.org).

Is your issue making sure that scientists remain free to research, invent, and thrive? Go to the National Center for Science Education, which defends the integrity of this field (www.ncse.com).

A newer issue that concerns many is net neutrality, or the concept that all Internet service providers (ISPs) should let everyone have access to all content and applications on the World Wide Web. You don't let the phone company decide to whom you should or should not talk, and neither, say net-neutrality advocates, should the ISPs decide what you can or cannot see. If this is your cause, then visit www.savetheinternet.com or the Electronic Frontier Foundation (www.eff.org). If Internet filtering and surveillance practices are your concern, the Open-Net Initiative will keep you up to speed on this issue (www.opennet.net).

Please don't forget that it's not just people who are going to be affected by the change in administration. Animals are just as influenced by policy decisions. There are many great organizations fighting to protect and help companion, farm, and/or wild animals. Some of the best include People for the Ethical Treatment of Animals (www.peta.org), the Humane League (www.thehumaneleague.com), Mercy for Animals (www.mercyforanimals.org), and the Humane Society of the United States (www.humanesociety.org).

There are also a number of good websites that can help you understand current events. There isn't room to list all of them here, but the following warrant a visit: Alternet (www .alternet.org), Crooks and Liars (www.crooksandliars.com), Daily Kos (dailykos.com), In These Times (www.inthesetimes. com), Mother Jones (www.motherjones.com), Raw Story (www .rawstory.com), Talking Points Memo (www.talkingpoints-memo.com), The Nation (www.thenation.com), Think Progress (www.thinkprogress.org), and Truthdig (www.truthdig .com).

These and other resources in each of this book's chapters give you a host of ways to fight back against Donald J. Trump. Use them. Make your voice heard. But there's one thing you might *not* want to do, and that is to help impeach him. Because standing next in line is Vice President–elect Mike Pence.

Who is Mike Pence? He is the governor of Indiana, a former lawyer, talk show host, and congressman from the state of Indiana (2001–2012). Most of his time in the House was spent fighting liberal social policy. Even George W. Bush was too liberal for him—he fought against increasing the minimum wage and the expansion of Medicare Part D. Pence voted against the Lilly Ledbetter Fair Pay Act, which calls for equal pay for women, three times. He opposed federal funding that would support treatment for people suffering from HIV and AIDS unless the government simultaneously invested in programs to discourage people from engaging in same-sex relationships.

As governor of Indiana, Mike Pence signed a bill that bans abortion sought because of genetic fetal abnormalities, and requires that miscarried or aborted fetuses be buried or cremated. (A federal judge blocked that law from taking effect.) Pence also gutted Planned Parenthood funding, which resulted in the closing of five of the provider's clinics in Indiana. He passed the nation's most rigorous so-called religious freedom laws, which critics feared would allow businesses to refuse service to gay men and women (a law so draconian that Indianans rose in revolt, forcing Pence to sign subsequent legislation aimed at addressing those fears).

Despite his Catholic upbringing, Pence went head-to-head with the Catholic Archdiocese of Indianapolis when he halted state support for efforts to relocate refugees, suggesting that refugees might be terrorists. He vowed to deport legally settled refugees as well. (The archdiocese welcomed a Syrian family into the city, regardless.)

Pence is also a climate change denier. He has a 4 percent National Environmental Scorecard rating from the League of

Conservation Voters. He also considers creationism a legitimate scientific theory that "was believed in by every signer of the Declaration of Independence."

So whereas we can't be sure what four years of Donald Trump will bring, we can guess all too well about the administration of Mike Pence.

Even so, we don't know what the future holds. At this point we can only conjecture. But more than working on an issue that concerns you, more than joining a demonstration, and more than signing a petition, perhaps the very best way to fight to keep this country a land of dignity and freedom is to show civility and support to all Americans, whatever their gender, race, creed, or color. When you buy your morning coffee from the Afghan man at the counter, or when you talk to the Puerto Rican woman who lives next door, or when you consult with your Estonian lawyer, or when you work with your South African accountant, tell them how much you appreciate what they do and how glad you are that they live here. Appoint yourself the ambassador for the America that you believe in.

ACKNOWLEDGMENTS

I'd like to thank Tetsuhiko Endo, Mark Langley, Mike Otterman, Kendra Pierre-Louis, Carl Pritzkat, and Miranda Spencer for their extraordinary efforts getting this book written and edited. Most of all, I'm indebted to Nicholas Bromley, whose talents are remarkable and whose patience is even more so. This book would not exist without his help.

At HarperCollins, I'd like to thank Matthew Daddona, who oversaw a difficult project with insight and intelligence. I'd also like to thank the rest of the team at Dey Street: Lynn Grady, Michael Barrs, Nyamekye Waliyaya, Andrea Molitor, Shelby Meizlik, Maureen Cole, Kendra Newton, Suet Chong, Mumtaz Mustafa, Jeanne Reina, Nicole Celli, David Palmer, Shelby Peak, Dale Rohrbaugh, Stephanie Vallejo, and all of those who treated this project with enthusiasm and urgency.

Also very helpful on this project were Nancy Averett, Gale Brewer, Paula Caplan, Jon Doyle, Steve Horn, Jill Kolasinksi, Ciara O'Rourke, Luke Shanahan, and Meaghan Wagner.

Finally, thank you, Chris Hays, for everything.

NOTES

CIVIL RIGHTS

1. http://fortune.com/2016/06/07/donald-trump-racism
   -quotes/
2. http://www.cnn.com/2016/03/23/politics/john-ehrlichman
   -richard-nixon-drug-war-blacks-hippie/
3. http://www.cnn.com/2016/07/18/politics/donald-trump
   -black-lives-matter/

THE ECONOMY

1. http://www.npr.org/2016/05/09/477350889/donald-trumps
   -messy-ideas-for-handling-the-national-debt-explained
2. http://www.politifact.com/truth-o-meter/article/2016
   /may/16/closer-look-donald-trumps-comments-about-refi
   nanci/?elqTrackId=0ad9d4b8ad304b35b960220471f84ff1&
   elq=a1bea2cc02bb48998928899154dfa3af&elqaid=31198&
   elqat=1&elqCampaignId=6206
3. http://www.nytimes.com/2016/05/07/us/politics/donald
   -trumps-idea-to-cut-national-debt-get-creditors-to-accept
   -less.html?_r=0

4. http://www.npr.org/2016/11/13/501739277/who-benefits -from-donald-trumps-tax-plan

5. http://www.realclearpolitics.com/video/2016/04/21 /trump_i_believe_in_raising_taxes_on_the_wealthy_includ ing_myself.html

6. http://www.npr.org/2016/11/13/501739277/who-benefits -from-donald-trumps-tax-plan

7. http://www.taxpolicycenter.org/publications/analysis-donald -trumps-revised-tax-plan/full

8. http://money.cnn.com/2016/10/17/pf/taxes/trump-tax-plan/

9. https://www.washingtonpost.com/news/wonk/wp/2016/09 /16/analysis-by-2025-99-6-of-paul-ryans-tax-cuts-would-go -to-the-richest-1-of-americans/

10. http://www.cnn.com/2016/11/15/politics/donald-trump -trade-memo-transition/index.html

11. http://www.politico.com/story/2016/06/donald-trump-trans -pacific-partnership-224916

12. http://money.cnn.com/2016/09/27/news/economy/donald -trump-nafta-hillary-clinton-debate/

13. http://money.cnn.com/2016/07/06/news/economy/trump -nafta/

14. http://www.bbc.com/news/world-latin-america-37945913

15. https://piie.com/system/files/documents/piieb16-6.pdf

EDUCATION

1. http://www.businessinsider.com/donald-trumps-2016-cam paign-ideas-2015-6

2. http://www.theatlantic.com/education/archive/2016/11/don ald-trump-on-education/507167/

3. http://eagnews.org/trump-eliminate-the-u-s-department-of -education/
4. http://www.usatoday.com/story/news/2016/11/23/5-things -know-trumps-education-secretary-pick-betsy-devos/94360110/
5. http://www.forbes.com/forbes/welcome/?toURL=http:// www.forbes.com/sites/emilywillingham/2016/11/24/trumps -education-secretary-choice-is-a-blow-to-our-nations-sci ence-health/&refURL=https://www.google.com/&referrer =https://www.google.com/
6. http://www.npr.org/sections/ed/2016/11/10/501426803/can -president-trump-get-rid-of-common-core

ENERGY

1. https://www.washingtonpost.com/news/the-fix/wp/2016 /05/26/theres-a-lot-to-unpack-in-donald-trumps-answers -about-energy-policy/
2. https://www.whitehouse.gov/blog/2014/05/29/new-report-all -above-energy-strategy-path-sustainable-economic-growth
3. https://www.washingtonpost.com/news/post-politics/wp /2015/11/03/seven-things-in-donald-trumps-new-book-you -probably-wont-hear-at-a-rally/

ENTITLEMENT PROGRAMS

1. https://www.donaldjtrump.com/media/why-donald-trump -wont-touch-your-entitlements
2. https://www.ssa.gov/history/locations.html
3. http://www.nytimes.com/2016/07/16/your-money/calls-for-so cial-security-expansion-grow-louder-in-washington.html?_r=0
4. https://www.washingtonpost.com/news/fact-checker/wp

/2016/11/14/paul-ryans-false-claim-that-because-of-obama care-medicare-is-going-broke/

5. http://www.forbes.com/sites/johnwasik/2016/11/16 /three-ways-trump-gop-may-cut-social-security-medicare /#88dad3f4e0e8

6. http://www.cnn.com/2016/03/10/politics/republican-debate -transcript-full-text/

7. http://bigstory.ap.org/article/9ffab80ebced434da0843e91cf 1192d6/trump-advisers-back-deregulation-privatized-social -security

8. http://wonkroom.thinkprogress.org/wp-content/uploads /2008/10/ss_report.pdf

9. https://www.greatagain.gov/policy/healthcare.html

10. https://www.washingtonpost.com/blogs/plum-line/wp/2016 /11/15/paul-ryans-plan-to-phase-out-medicare-is-just-what -democrats-need/?utm_term=.0d3087677355

11. https://www.greatagain.gov/policy/healthcare.html

12. http://www.npr.org/2011/03/08/134363543/gop-governors -revive-historic-call-for-medicaid-block-grants

ENVIRONMENT

1. http://www.politifact.com/truth-o-meter/statements/2016 /jun/03/hillary-clinton/yes-donald-trump-did-call-climate -change-chinese-h/

2. http://www.cnsnews.com/news/article/obama-predicts-sub merged-countries-abandoned-cities-fields-no-longer-grow

3. http://www.cnbc.com/2016/11/09/regulation-buster-trump -takes-aim-at-the-epa.html

4. http://fortune.com/2016/10/19/debate-trump/

5. http://www.vanityfair.com/news/2007/05/skeptic200705

6. http://environment.harvard.edu/news/faculty-news/implica tions-trump-victory-energyclimate-policy

IMMIGRATION

1. https://www.washingtonpost.com/news/fact-checker/wp /2015/07/08/donald-trumps-false-comments-connecting -mexican-immigrants-and-crime/
2. http://www.peerallylaw.com/en/content/view/214
3. https://www.whitehouse.gov/the-press-office/2016/06/23 /remarks-president-supreme-court-decision-us-versus-texas
4. http://www.cnn.com/2015/11/11/politics/donald-trump-de portation-force-debate-immigration/
5. http://www.nytimes.com/2016/11/15/us/politics/donald -trump-deport-immigrants.html?_r=0
6. https://www.washingtonpost.com/news/the-fix/wp/2015/11/11 /donald-trump-endorsed-operation-wetback-but-not-by-name/
7. https://www.washingtonpost.com/news/morning-mix/wp /2016/11/17/japanese-internment-is-precedent-for-national -muslim-registry-prominent-trump-backer-says/
8. http://www.npr.org/2016/11/09/501451368/here-is-what-don ald-trump-wants-to-do-in-his-first-100-days
9. https://www.washingtonpost.com/video/politics/trump-says -he-will-build-impenetrable-physical-tall-powerful-beautiful -border/2016/08/31/34eceacc-6fb6-11e6-993f-73c693a89820 _video.html

LGBTQ ISSUES

1. http://www.cbsnews.com/pictures/wild-donald-trump -quotes/17/

NATIONAL SECURITY

1. http://www.cbsnews.com/news/face-the-nation-transcripts-march-6-2016-trump-cruz-clinton-priebus/
2. http://avalon.law.yale.edu/18th_century/washing.asp
3. http://www.washingtonpost.com/wp-dyn/content/blog/2006/06/19/BL2006061900578.html
4. http://www.huffingtonpost.com/2009/05/11/ig-report-water boarding-w_n_201733.html
5. http://usatoday30.usatoday.com/news/washington/2006-05-10-nsa_x.htm
6. http://www.msnbc.com/msnbc/bush-trump-spar-over-george-w-bushs-legacy
7. http://www.bloomberg.com/politics/videos/2016-04-27/trump-it-s-time-to-shake-the-rust-off-america-s-foreign-policy
8. https://www.donaldjtrump.com/press-releases/donald-j.-trump-foreign-policy-speech
9. http://www.politifact.com/truth-o-meter/statements/2016/aug/16/donald-trump/donald-trump-mischaracterizes-nato-change-and-his-/
10. http://miamiherald.typepad.com/nakedpolitics/2016/08/trump-revisits-guantánamo-question-says-foreigners-would-be-tried-there.html
11. http://www.npr.org/sections/parallels/2016/11/14/502007304/trump-has-vowed-to-fill-guantanamo-with-some-bad-dudes-but-who
12. https://www.washingtonpost.com/politics/trump-says-tor ture-works-backs-waterboarding-and-much-worse/2016/02/17/4c9277be-d59c-11e5-b195-2e29a4e13425_story.html
13. https://www.washingtonpost.com/world/national-security

/trumps-pick-for-national-security-adviser-brings-experience-and-controversy/2016/11/17/0962eb88-ad08-11e6-8b45-f8e493f06fcd_story.html

14. http://www.politico.com/story/2016/07/trump-law-order-candidate-225372

15. http://www.cnn.com/2016/07/18/politics/donald-trump-black-lives-matter/

16. http://www.cnn.com/2015/11/21/politics/trump-muslims-surveillance/

17. http://www.cnn.com/2016/11/22/politics/kfile-michael-flynn-august-speech/

18. https://www.washingtonpost.com/world/national-security/iran-nuclear-deal-could-collapse-under-trump/2016/11/09/f2d2bd02-a68c-11e6-ba59-a7d93165c6d4_story.html

19. https://twitter.com/RepMikePompeo/status/799266269853863937

OBAMACARE

1. https://www.washingtonpost.com/news/post-politics/wp/2015/08/07/the-three-biggest-donald-trump-flip-flops-in-thursdays-debate/

2. https://twitter.com/realdonaldtrump/status/794155725152980992

3. http://www.weeklystandard.com/trump-i-like-obamacares-individual-mandate/article/2001172

4. https://www.donaldjtrump.com/positions/healthcare-reform

5. http://www.usnews.com/news/articles/2016-03-03/trump-health-care-plan-would-repeal-obamacare-examine-mental-health

6. http://www.wsj.com/articles/donald-trump-willing-to-keep
   -parts-of-health-law-1478895339
7. http://money.cnn.com/2016/11/28/news/economy/tom-price
   -trump-health-secretary/index.html?adkey=bn
8. https://cdn.americanprogress.org/wp-content/uploads/issues
   /2010/08/pdf/repealing_reform.pdf
9. http://www.forbes.com/sites/brucelee/2016/11/14/in-60
   -minutes-interview-heres-what-trump-said-about-healthcare
   /#47f52ec3533f
10. http://dfw.cbslocal.com/2015/09/14/trump-america-a-dump
    ing-ground-for-the-rest-of-the-world/

POLITICAL ISSUES

1. https://twitter.com/realdonaldtrump/status/7858287724235
   61216?lang=en
2. http://www.politico.com/blogs/south-carolina-primary-2016
   -live-updates-and-results/2016/02/gop-debate-2016-trump
   -911-219260
3. http://www.slate.com/blogs/the_slatest/2016/11/18/jeff_ses
   sions_is_trump_s_pick_for_attorney_general.html
4. http://bigstory.ap.org/article/93d1908f2a324c3492dd117f17
   12b14e/trump-wrongly-insists-voter-fraud-very-very-common
5. https://www.washingtonpost.com/news/the-fix/wp/2016
   /10/18/no-1-8-million-dead-people-arent-going-to-vote-in
   -november/

WOMEN'S ISSUES

1. http://bigstory.ap.org/article/2eea389b1e5b49f8afb28c4a6
   d079b09/some-donald-trumps-most-insulting-comments
   -about-women

2. https://www.whitehouse.gov/the-press-office/2014/08/26
   /fact-sheet-obama-administration-record-women-and-girls

3. http://www.msnbc.com/all-in/watch/nobody-has-more-re
   spect-for-women-than-i-do-790490179874

4. http://www.cnn.com/2016/06/02/politics/trump-wife-com
   ments-abc-interview/

5. http://www.cnn.com/2016/09/08/politics/donald-trump-mil
   itary-sexual-assault/

6. https://www.washingtonpost.com/politics/trump-recorded
   -having-extremely-lewd-conversation-about-women-in-2005
   /2016/10/07/3b9ce776-8cb4-11e6-bf8a-3d26847eeed4_story
   .html

7. http://www.cnn.com/2015/07/29/politics/trump-breast
   -pump-statement/

8. http://www.huffingtonpost.com/entry/alicia-machado-don
   ald-trump_us_57431d11e4b00e09e89f8aa4

9. http://www.npr.org/2016/10/20/498736807/women-on-social
   -media-respond-to-trump-calling-clinton-a-nasty-woman

10. https://www.washingtonpost.com/news/post-politics/wp
    /2015/08/07/trump-says-foxs-megyn-kelly-had-blood-coming
    -out-of-her-wherever/

11. http://www.nytimes.com/2016/03/31/us/politics/donald
    -trump-abortion.html?_r=0

12. http://www.cbsnews.com/news/60-minutes-donald-trump
    -family-melania-ivanka-lesley-stahl/

HOW TO CONTACT YOUR REPRESENTATIVES

Contacting your elected representatives can seem daunting, but it is the single best way to make your voice heard.

First, always call. Using social media and email is fine, but online communication is often ignored. It is much easier for your representatives' offices to tally phone calls than to sift through emails and tweets, and calling ensures that your concerns are received.

Start by contacting your representatives in the House and Senate. Use their district phone line first, and then their D.C. line. House members in particular are receptive to their local constituents. District lines also tend to be less busy than the D.C. offices, and you will be speaking with a staffer who knows your local community well. Beyond your own representatives, party leadership and representatives serving on issue-related committees are also excellent options for outreach.

Always be polite. In most cases you will be speaking with a staffer, and if you are rude, he or she is less likely to pass on your message. Begin with a compliment, especially if you are asking your officials to take a divisive position on an issue.

Here is a simple script you can use as a template:

Hello, my name is [full name] a constituent from [City, State] calling to share some of my concerns about [issue] with the Senator/Congress(wo)man. First, I'd like to thank the Senator/Congress(wo)man for [compliment, e.g.: their service to our state].

I am calling today to share my concerns about [issue], which is a problem because [reason why this issue should be of concern and share how the problem affects you personally, if applicable]. I ask the Senator/Congress(wo)man [action to address your concern].

Thank you very much for taking time to speak with me.

You can adapt this script for each issue, but always be sure to end your call with a concrete call to action, even if it is simply asking that your representatives keep your concerns in mind. After a week, you can follow up. Remember, be persistent, but polite.

For a detailed database of who your elected officials are, what their contact information is, and what bills they have sponsored, visit http://www.commoncause.org.